AGENDA FOR SOCIAL JUSTICE

Solutions for 2020

Edited by
Glenn W. Muschert, Kristen M. Budd,
Michelle Christian, and Robert Perrucci

T0339279

P

First published in Great Britain in 2020 by

Policy Press
University of Bristol
1–9 Old Park Hill
Bristol
BS2 8BB
UK
t: +44 (0)117 954 5940
pp-info@bristol.ac.uk
www.policypress.co.uk

British Library Cataloguing in Publication Data
A catalogue record for this book is available from the British Library

ISBN 978-1-4473-5428-4 paperback
ISBN 978-1-4473-5461-1 ePdf

The right of Glenn W. Muschert, Kristen M. Budd, Michelle Christian, and Robert Perrucci
to be identified as editors of this work has been asserted by them in accordance with the
Copyright, Designs and Patents Act 1988.

Cover design by Clifford Hayes
Front cover image: Handprint © Freepik.com
Printed and bound in Great Britain by CMP, Poole
Policy Press uses environmentally responsible print partners

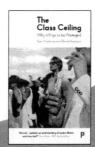

Table of Contents

President's Welcome

Heather Dalmage

As an organization, the Society for the Study of Social Problems (SSSP) has a membership that is well-versed in a myriad of specific and broad problems facing the world. With the complexity and onslaught of crises worldwide, we can all be tempted to throw up our arms and get lost in a Netflix series, but as a social justice organization grounded in social science, we do not have that option. Instead, we engage in work that creates solutions toward a more just world. The SSSP was created and is sustained by individuals who have identified solutions to social problems. We are an organization of scholars who create dreams of transformation, guided and built upon our sociological imagination and research, sense of hope in humanity, and a belief in our ability to create change. We mobilize our sociological research and insight to inform policy and activism that will lead to the creation of more just worlds. Imagine for a moment, we could easily be the Society for the Study of Social Solutions! On behalf of the SSSP, I am honored to invite you to read the *Agenda for Social Justice: Solutions for 2020* and to thank Glenn Muschert and his team for their work on this superb volume.

Editorial Introduction

Glenn W. Muschert and Kristen M. Budd

> "Doing sociology at this crucial time of our history, we need to be social activists and sociology must be engaged in social justice ... Sociological data is wasted if our studies fail to affect public understandings of social issues or if research is not applied to improving social conditions."
>
> –Mary Romero

The volume you are reading, *Agenda for Social Justice*, was directly inspired by the 2000 Presidential Address delivered by Professor Robert Perrucci, the 48th President of the Society for the Study of Social Problems (SSSP). During the annual meetings held in August in Washington, DC, Dr. Perrucci outlined his criticism of the scholarship produced by SSSP members and other social scientists, indicating that over time its focus had drifted toward the abstract and intellectual, and away from the concrete social justice work to solve social problems which has inspired the Society's foundation and the scholarship of its earliest members. Because of this, Dr. Perrucci warned, sociology and related disciplines had become less relevant in public discourse, and this crisis of legitimacy was echoed in policy-making circles, as much social research was ignored in policy debates, and rather sat upon the dusty shelves of academic libraries (and now perhaps in similarly unread corners of academic databases).

To remedy this, Dr. Perrucci called for SSSP members to produce a "report to the nation" whose issuance would coincide with major elections in the U.S. These reports, Dr. Perrucci said, should define significant social problems facing the nation, explain via best available data and research the extent of such problems, and propose practicable policy solutions which can mitigate or solve these social problems. The vision was that the SSSP membership would periodically produce a volume which would be based on the best research evidence available, but which would be written in jargon-free language accessible to the general public and "to get people in the wider society thinking about the 'middle range utopias' that could serve as alternatives" to the contemporary snarl of social problems.

Dr. Perrucci's speech was the keynote address of the 50th Annual Meeting of the SSSP, the first of the new millennium, organized under the theme "Inventing Social Justice: SSSP and the 21st Century." Indeed, this speech was among the first to advocate for a return to studying the dynamics of concrete problems and their solution, and seems to have served as an inspiration more broadly by setting the public sociology agenda that has been observed since in the SSSP and beyond. From this inspiration, a new committee was formed, the Justice 21 Committee, whose mission has been to advance the injection of rigorous sociology into public discourse, and to increase the practical applicability of social science research concerning social problems.

The first volumes of the *Agenda for Social Justice* were self-published in hard copy by the Justice 21 Committee in 2004 and 2008, and the 2012 volume was published in e-book and print-on-demand versions. Since 2016, the volume has been published by Policy Press, our academic publisher based at the University of Bristol (UK) whose values closely align with those of the Justice 21 Committee and the SSSP as a whole. In forging a relationship with our publisher, we now contribute directly to Policy Press's mission "to encourage problem-centered social research and to foster cooperative relations among persons and organizations engaged in the application of scientific sociological findings to the formulation of social policies." We further partnered with Policy Press, starting in 2018, to publish the internationally-focused *Global Agenda for Social Justice*, which is planned to appear in the even-numbered years between the major U.S. election years. We also point out that Policy Press graciously provides hard copies for distribution to SSSP Annual Meeting attendees, and allows us to post copies of both the U.S.-focused and global-focused volumes for open access download worldwide on the Society's web page. Tracking of IP addresses of downloads indicate that our volumes have been downloaded literally around the world, which although perhaps not precisely the impact Dr. Perrucci envisioned in his 2000 speech, is nonetheless an indication of the project's worldwide impact.

This volume includes 16 topical chapters examining some of the most pressing social problems facing America in these times, and one "think piece" intended to spark rumination on the topic of social problems more generally.[1] Our contributors draw upon a vast array of experiences, but each brings their academic work forward with the intention of using rigorous scholarship to develop practical policies to mitigate or solve a significant social problem. Those who have contributed to this volume have vast experience indeed. The chapters are contributed by 26 scholars from various public and private academic institutions, and this impressive and diverse group of social science researchers and policy analysts consists of graduate students, postdoctoral researchers, and university faculty at all levels: Assistant, Associate, Full, and Emeritus Professors. Among the group are some Endowed Chairs and Directors affiliated with social science departments and prestigious research institutes, including a past President of the SSSP (1991–92). Contributor biographical sketches appear at the beginning of the book, but unfortunately our limited space does not allow the inclusion of a list of the numerous research articles and books written and/or edited by our contributors, many of whom are extremely prolific.

The academic chapter is the dispassionate medium we use here to convey concern about significant social problems, and our best expression of the practical desire to see such problems reduced or solved. While our writing may at times be detached, please understand that the contributors to this volume, and indeed SSSP members more generally, are indeed very passionate about their work. Case in point is our longtime colleague Robert Aponte, whose chapter on "Police Homicides" appears in this volume. Dr. Aponte was a veteran social justice scholar whose involvement with the SSSP stretched across many decades. We are saddened that, shortly after submitting the final version of his chapter, our colleague Robert passed away. He will be missed sorely by those who have worked beside him, and indeed by those who looked to him as a role model. In the months leading up to the production of this volume, Robert faced notable health challenges, and went through difficult treatments. Even though he quite gracefully could have abandoned the idea of contributing a chapter to this volume, he nonetheless remained committed to writing and revising his chapter. Robert did this because of his deep commitment to social justice scholarship and evidence-based social action. Simply stated, for an extended period he had been mulling over the injustice of police homicides in America, and he wrote this chapter as an expression of his commitment to social justice and to truth telling. This is who Dr. Robert Aponte was as a scholar and a person, one whose commitment to social research and social action transcended substantial personal difficulties. While we grieve the loss of Robert, our brother sociologist, we see his inspiration in ourselves and those with whom we share our struggle for social justice. Although we may speak dispassionately about grave injustices, and though we may conduct rigorous research using methods designed to be detached, so many of us recognize that such work comes from the heart, just as Robert's chapter here was something that was unambiguously close to his heart.

Indeed, each of the chapters in this year's *Agenda for Social Justice* is contributed by a scholar whose topic is close to their heart. Each contributor is an outstanding scholar in their respective sub-fields, and each piece addresses a specific social problem facing the U.S. today. Each chapter can stand on its own, and it would be possible to select single chapters for reading and discussion in classrooms, coffee shops, community meetings, or other fora where social problems are discussed. Note also that chapters follow a format that divides the content into three major sections: the first defining the social problem, the second providing evidence available to describe the extent of the problem, and the third offering concrete suggestions for the policies to ameliorate these problems. Each chapter also includes a list of key resources for anyone wanting a further look into each respective problem. The final chapter and the Afterword are written in a different style and are meant to be pieces that take a broader view of social problems in general, with an eye toward the pursuit of social justice.

The materials presented in this volume cover a wide variety of topics ranging from race/ethnicity, family policies, healthcare, sexual harassment, education issues, crime/justice, environment, and employment. We have grouped these chapters into imperfect section titles that give an indication of overlapping and intersecting issues, that we hope are meaningful. It is appropriate to mention to our readers that the *Agenda for Social Justice* is not designed to be a comprehensive list of social problems in America today, but rather a reflection of the significant issues proposed by our contributors. In soliciting chapters, we put out a call for proposals and then selected from the pool of submissions received. Noticeably absent from the submissions, for example, were a number of pressing issues such as white supremacy, economic inequality, mass violence, and the perennial involvement of the U.S. in foreign wars. Nonetheless, the social issues included are broad-ranging and certainly among the most pressing social justice issues facing the United States today. It is the Justice 21 Committee's hope that this book as a whole and the individual chapters will provide information and great utility to students, policy makers, researchers, and the general public. Please take the enclosed research, arguments, and solutions into discussions in your classrooms and other venues, and use them as a point of discussion among your peers, especially if you share our vision of social justice to inspire corrective actions for the social problems in America, ultimately creating a more inclusive, equitable, healthy, peaceful, and just society.

Electronic copies of all volumes of the *Agenda for Social Justice* are available for open access download at: https://www.sssp1.org/index.cfm/m/771/locationSectionId/0/Agenda_for_Social_Justice.

Electronic copies of the *Global Agenda for Social Justice* are similarly available for open access download at: https://www.sssp1.org/index. cfm/m/323/locationSectionId/0/Global_Agenda_for_Social_Justice.

Note

[1] The submissions for the volume were completed prior to the global dispersion of COVID-19. We are currently in the process of facilitating a new edited volume on the vast social injustices COVID-19 accentuates and is creating.

Key Resources

Romero, M. (2020). Sociology engaged in social justice. *American Sociological Review, 85*(1), 1–30. doi: 10.1177/0003122419893677

Acknowledgments

This volume would not have been possible without the cooperation and support of so many good people. We (the editors) wish to thank our authors first, for working with us and for their quality contributions. It is a pleasure to work with such a group of professionals to bring ideas to print. As always, we are indebted to Michele Koontz and Héctor Delgado of the SSSP administrative and executive offices, respectively, for their support and encouragement. We thank acquisitions editor Victoria Pittman and her team at Policy Press, with whom we are pleased to collaborate on this book. We thank our colleague Sadia Jamil for her editorial and moral support. Finally, we thank all our fellow students, scholars, and activists who make the SSSP such an exciting environment in which to study, research, write, and undertake meaningful social action.

Finally, this volume is dedicated to the memory of our colleague Dr. Robert Aponte.

About the Society for the Study of Social Problems

The Society for the Study of Social Problems (the SSSP), is an academic and action-oriented professional association, whose purpose is to promote and protect social science research and teaching about significant social problems in society. Members of the SSSP include students, faculty members at educational institutions, researchers, practitioners, and advocates.

Some of the SSSP's core activities include encouraging rigorous research, nurturing young sociologists, focusing on solutions to the problems of society, fostering cooperative relations between the academic and the policy and/or social action spheres.

If you would like to learn more about joining the SSSP, reading our publications, or attending our annual conference, please visit the SSSP website: www.sssp1.org.

Finally, please consider supporting the SSSP, a nonprofit 501(c) 3 organization which accepts tax deductible contributions both in support of its general operations and for specific purposes. It is possible to donate to the SSSP in general, but it is also possible to donate in support of specific efforts. If you would like to encourage the kind of public sociology represented in this book, please consider supporting the efforts of the Justice 21 Committee. For information on contributing, please visit www.sssp1.org/index.cfm/m/584/.

Notes on Contributors

Robert Aponte (1947–2020) received his Ph.D. in sociology from the University of Chicago. He was Associate Professor of Sociology at IUPUI where he served as Department Chair from 2003 to 2010. He co-founded the IUPUI Latino Studies Program. His specializations included social justice issues related to Latin American immigration, poverty and drug policy, and race and ethnicity. His publications have appeared in such journals as *Social Problems*, the *Global Agenda for Social Justice*, the *Latino Studies Journal*, *Journal of Latino-Latin American Studies*, *Race and Human Rights*, *Omega Journal of Death and Dying*, and the *International Journal of Sociology and Social Policy*.

Aneesa A. Baboolal is Assistant Professor in the Department of Crime and Justice Studies at the University of Massachusetts–Dartmouth. Her research interests include gender-based violence across intersecting identities including, race/ethnicity, immigrant, and religious minority status. Her recent work examines how Muslim students respond to gendered and racialized violence in the United States during the Trump era.

Bianca E. Bersani, Ph.D., is Associate Professor of Criminology and Criminal Justice at the University of Maryland, College Park. She holds a Ph.D. in criminology and criminal justice from the University of Maryland (2010) and is a 2011 W.E.B. Du Bois Fellow of the National Institute of Justice. Her research involves the study of the generational disparity in immigrant offending; patterns and predictors of offending over the life course; desistance and persistence in offending; family and intimate relationship dynamics; divergence in offending across race/ethnicity, gender, and immigration status; and the application of innovative methodologies to understand the mechanisms of behavioral change.

Sarah Jane Brubaker, Ph.D., is a Professor of Criminal Justice and Public Policy at the L. Douglas Wilder School of Government and Public Affairs at Virginia Commonwealth University, where she directs a Certificate in Gender Violence Intervention. A sociologist by training, Dr. Brubaker conducts research on sexual assault and other forms of gender violence, juvenile justice, and adolescent sexual health. Her current projects include transdisciplinary and community-engaged research approaches to expanding access to oral health care to urban children and disrupting the criminalization of trauma through exclusionary discipline of African American children in urban schools.

Kristen M. Budd, Ph.D., is Associate Professor of Sociology and Criminology at Miami University, Oxford. She holds a Ph.D. in sociology from Purdue University (2011), with a specialization in law and society. Her research focuses on interpersonal violence, law, and policy including how they intersect with perpetrator and victim sociodemographic characteristics. Currently, she researches patterns and predictors of offending behavior in relation to sexual assault; public perceptions in relation to criminal behavior, law, and criminal justice policy and practice; and social and legal responses to interpersonal violence and other social problems.

Ronald E. Bulanda, Ph.D., is Associate Professor of Sociology at Miami University. He earned a Ph.D. in sociology from Bowling Green State University in 2004 with a major in family sociology and a minor in social psychology. His research interests include a focus on family structures, parenting, and child well-being.

Wayne Centrone is a physician and public health professional who has dedicated his career to working with high risk and marginalized homeless and underserved populations around the world. Wayne is the Founder and President of Health Bridges International and serves as Senior Health Advisor with C4 Innovations.

Michelle Christian is Associate Professor at the University of Tennessee, Knoxville. Her research specialty areas are critical race, global political economy, and precarious forms of work. She has conducted research projects in the United States, Central America, and East Africa.

LaTrice L. Dowtin, Ph.D., LCPC, NCSP, RPT, is a specialist-level nationally certified school psychologist and a licensed clinical professional counselor with advanced training in clinical psychology. She specializes in trauma and infant/perinatal mental health for culturally, racially, and linguistically diverse people. Dr. Dowtin is a published author, public speaker, and trainer on topics regarding racial and cultural inequities and socioemotional development. She has worked with people of all ages, school leaders, and hospitals in regions across the United States for the over 15 years. Dr. Dowtin stands firm in her determination to promote social justice and decrease racial inequities for Black children by fostering excellence within Black communities.

Cherrell Green, M.A., is a doctoral candidate in the Department of Criminology and Criminal Justice at the University of Missouri– St. Louis. Her work centers on examining two broad areas: the intersection of race/ethnicity, crime and criminal justice; and the intersection of urban violence and trauma over the life-course.

R. Neil Greene is a Ph.D. candidate in the Sociology Department at the University of New Mexico. He teaches research methods at UNM, is an Evaluator with Apex Evaluation, and is a member of the Program Review Committee within the Albuquerque Healthcare for the Homeless program.

Hannah Hurrle completed her B.A. in sociology and philosophy at IUPUI, where she is currently working on her Sociology M.A. Her areas of interest are in social justice issues related to race and ethnicity, drug policy, poverty, disability, and mental illness.

Sadia Jamil is a postdoctoral fellow at Khalifa University of Science and Technology, Abu Dhabi, UAE. She received her Ph.D, in journalism at the University of Queensland, Australia in 2015. She also holds postgraduate degrees in the disciplines of media management (University of Stirling, Scotland) and mass communication (University of Karachi). Dr Jamil is currently serving as the Co Vice-Chair of the Journalism Research and Education Section of the IAMCR.

Sujatha A. Jesudason, Ph.D., is Professor of Professional Practice in Management at The New School and has more than 25 years of experience of working in social movements. Her work ranges from community organizing in Milwaukee to violence prevention in the South Asian community, to the social justice implications of genetic technologies. A serial social justice entrepreneur, she was the founder and executive director of Generations Ahead and CoreAlign where she brought together leaders from several different movements to strategize and innovate into the future. Currently, at The New School, she teaches classes in Re-imagining Social Movements, Speaking Race to Power, and Leadership for Social Innovation. She is the founder and Faculty Director of the Social Movements + Innovation Lab, a space to explore and test disruptive social movement strategies. Sujatha earned her M.A. and Ph.D. in sociology at the University of California, Berkeley and her undergraduate degrees in economics and Latin American studies at the University of Wisconsin–Madison.

Arne L. Kalleberg is Kenan Distinguished Professor of Sociology at the University of North Carolina at Chapel Hill. He has published extensively on topics related to the sociology of work, organizations, occupations and industries, labor markets, and social stratification. His most recent book is *Precarious Lives: Job Insecurity and Well-Being in Rich Democracies* (Polity Press, 2018). Other current projects include studies of mobility out of low-wage jobs in the United States; and the politics of precarious work in Japan, South Korea, and Indonesia. He served as the President of the American Sociological Association in 2007–8 and is currently the editor of *Social Forces*, an international journal of social research.

Brittany Keegan, Ph.D., is the research coordinator and director of the Land Use Education Program at Virginia Commonwealth University's Center for Public Policy. Her research examines the role of nonprofits in supporting those impacted by violence and/or conflict, with a primary focus on refugee and immigrant populations and those impacted by gender-based violence. Recent and ongoing projects include an evaluation of the effectiveness and responsiveness of nonprofits in promoting refugee integration, and the creation of training programs related to achieving housing equity for marginalized populations.

Bronwen Lichtenstein, Ph.D., is Professor of Sociology in the Department of Criminology and Criminal Justice at The University of Alabama. Her research on the sociology of health and illness has led to numerous journal articles relating to health disparities in the Deep South. Other areas of research include women's financial well-being over the life course, gender–race inequities in housing loss, and family law reform in the United States. Dr. Lichtenstein is the principal investigator of longitudinal research on the social impacts of foreclosure, a women's health study, and a program for HIV and hepatitis-C services for community corrections.

Sadé L. Lindsay, M.A., is a Ph.D. candidate in sociology at the Ohio State University and a Ruth D. Peterson Fellow of the American Society of Criminology. Her research interests include punishment and inequality, incarceration and reentry, and drug use. Sadé's National Science Foundation-funded dissertation examines how prison job training impacts post-incarceration employment. Her research has been published in the *Journal of Research in Crime and Delinquency* and *The Prison Journal*. In addition to research, Sadé prepares young men at an Ohio juvenile correctional facility for reentry and helps advance their educational goals.

Glenn W. Muschert is Professor of Sociology in the Department of Humanities and Social Sciences at Khalifa University of Science and Technology, Abu Dhabi, UAE. He previously served on the Faculty of Sociology and Social Justice Studies at Miami University, Ohio. His research focuses on digital technologies, sustainable development, and the ethical solution of social problems worldwide.

David N. Pellow is the Dehlsen Chair and Professor of Environmental Studies and Director of the Global Environmental Justice Project at the University of California, Santa Barbara. His teaching, research, and activism focus on environmental justice in the U.S. and globally. His books include *What is Critical Environmental Justice?*; *The Slums of Aspen: Immigrants vs. the Environment in America's Eden* (with Lisa Sun-Hee Park); *The Silicon Valley of Dreams: Environmental Injustice, Immigrant Workers, and the High-Tech Global Economy* (with Lisa Sun-Hee Park); and *Garbage Wars: The Struggle for Environmental Justice in Chicago*. He has served on the Boards of Directors of Greenpeace USA and International Rivers.

Stephen Pfohl, Ph.D., is Professor of Sociology at Boston College where he teaches courses on social theory, visual cultural studies, critical criminology, deviance and social control, and social psychoanalysis. The author of numerous works, including *Predicting Dangerousness, Death at the Parasite Café, Images of Deviance and Social Control, Left Behind: Religion, Technology and Flight from the Flesh*, the co-edited *Culture, Power, and History*, and "The 'Discovery' of Child Abuse." A past president of the Society for the Study of Social Problems, Stephen is currently completing a two-volume study of "social suggestion" and cybernetic forms of power.

Amelia Pittman is a graduate student in the Department of Sociology and Gerontology at Miami University. Her research focuses on social determinants of health across the life course, as well as the impact of social policy on health. She was awarded a bachelor's degree in sociology from Miami University in May 2019, and is now pursuing her Masters of Gerontological Studies degree.

Sylvia Puente is the Executive Director of the Latino Policy Forum. She was named one of the Chicago's most powerful Latinos by Crain's Chicago Business. She earned a B.A. in economics from the University of Illinois at Urbana–Champaign. She did graduate studies at Harvard Kennedy School of Government and earned her Master's degree from the Harris School of Public Policy at the University of Chicago. She has been a member of gubernatorial and mayoral transition teams and is often called upon by local, state, and national leaders to provide leadership on issues related to education, housing, and immigration. She was one of 25 Chicago area women named a "Pioneer for Social Justice."

Jennifer Roebuck Bulanda is Associate Professor in the Department of Sociology and Gerontology at Miami University. Her research interests include family demography, relationship dynamics, health and well-being, and the sociology of aging. She teaches courses on social forces and aging, demography, introductory sociology, and medical sociology, focusing on issues such as population and health trends, relationships across the life course, and the social determinants of health.

Mawule A. Sevon, M.A., NCSP, BCBA, has worked with children and families across the city of Philadelphia and the District of Columbia's metropolitan areas for well over a decade. She has earned recognition for her unique contributions to the fields of education and social justice. Having a specialist degree in school psychology and certification as a behavior analyst, she uses her behavioral approach to impact disparities in the educational system. The issue that has most captured her attention and catalyzed the focus of her professional practice is the glaring racial inequity in how disciplinary action is applied across schools in the United States.

Noreen M. Sugrue is currently a research fellow at the Latino Policy Forum. She is a sociologist and a former faculty member in the Women and Gender in Global Perspective program at the University of Illinois at Urbana–Champaign. Her research and policy work are centered on issues of inequality and inequity. She has conducted research related to immigration, immigrants, health care, and workforce issues. Her work has been published in both academic and popular press venues.

SECTION I

Ethnicity, Race, and Gender

ONE

Islamophobia

Aneesa A. Baboolal

The Problem

Islamophobia as fear, hatred, and prejudice against Muslims is a form of racism that results in religious intolerance, persecution, and ethnic profiling. Islamophobia in the United States is rooted in notions of orientalism and presumptions of inherent violent behavior which uphold tropes of Muslim men as terrorists and women as oppressed. Islamophobia exists at both the interpersonal level, wherein suspicion of Muslims is normalized, and structurally, as violence against Muslim communities is linked to state-enforced policies such as those implemented after September 11, 2001. Examples of such policies include the National Security Entry-Exit Registration System[1] (NSEERS; colloquially known as the first Muslim Registry), Countering Violent Extremism (CVE),[2] policing via War on Terror initiatives such as the USA Patriot Act (2002)[3] and the NYPD Muslim Surveillance Program,[4] as well as advances for both the National Security Agency and US Foreign Intelligence, including warrantless surveillance of telecommunications and expansion of the obtaining and sharing of information on US citizens and foreigners.

Up to eight months after 9/11, Muslims reported discrimination that included FBI raids of religious organizations, damage to mosques, vandalism to businesses, racial/ethnic profiling, verbal harassment, and physical violence. In addition, various non-Muslim ethnic minority and diaspora communities were impacted by surveillance and discrimination with a total of more than 1,700 acts of hate violence toward those "appearing to be of Arab/South Asian descent" occurring after September 11. During this period, predominantly Muslim ethnic enclaves across the US experienced a crisis of citizenship[5] linked to changing government policies, increasingly restrictive immigration regulations (including mass deportations), scrutiny by law enforcement officials (such as increased surveillance) and the reinforcement of citizen surveillance, which resulted in an Islamophobic backlash linked to bias crimes, hate speech, and internal community changes.

Mechanisms of citizen surveillance impacted vulnerable groups via stigmatization, racial profiling, and interference with religious freedom, while damaging law enforcement and minority community relations. In recent years, political rhetoric and policies (such as Trump's travel ban), are reflective of the normalization of prejudice towards racial/ethnic and religious minority groups, Islamophobia is inextricably linked to other social inequalities, including immigration, anti-Black racism, racial/ethnic and religious profiling, and violence against Muslim women.

Overall, the 2016 US Presidential Election had a sweeping effect on marginalized groups in the US via xenophobia and Islamophobia. Studies indicate that the election was characterized by prejudice toward marginalized groups, which were targeted by political rhetoric and campaign slogans that promoted a climate of acceptable prejudice that resulted in an increase in bias incidents. The Southern Poverty Law Center described the implications of discriminatory and divisive political rhetoric on marginalized people during this period as "the Trump Effect." This period, also colloquially referred to as the Trump Era, saw elevated levels of discrimination toward immigrants, increased fears of deportation, and emboldened expressions of politicized bullying. On January 27, 2017, days into the Trump presidency, Executive Order No. 13769, known as the "travel ban" or "Muslim ban", was issued under the guise of national security. It subsequently prohibited foreign nationals from seven predominantly Muslim countries from entering the United States for 90 days, including visa and green-card holders, and the indefinite suspension of entry by Syrian refugees. The "Muslim ban" ultimately upheld Islamophobic U.S. policy and had an impact on Muslim immigrants and Muslim Americans, while also exacerbating fears. Given the immediate impact on the Muslim community, scholars argue that "Make America great again" was a vision for the country that further demonized Islam, which was supported by campaign rhetoric that included statements from Trump such as "I think Islam hates us" and his call for a "total and complete shutdown of Muslims entering the United States", which ultimately resulted in the Muslim Ban.

Muslims are viewed as Arab or a monolithic Middle Eastern group, thus resulting in stereotypes about various diverse communities. Historical notions of Arabs, and subsequently of Muslims, as 'other', inferior, violent, and savage, as a result of stereotypes of all Middle Easterners as Muslim, further dehumanized large groups of people who are seen as being opposed to progressive Western values. This broad generalization of Muslims stems from post-9/11 stigma that resulted in the racialization of religion linked to political, cultural, and social factors in society. Muslim religious identity has taken on racial meanings and become synonymous with notions of a 'threat to national security', a process that has resulted in the increased surveillance of brown bodies in public spaces and a denial of citizenship privileges. The racialization of religious identity also means that non-Muslims can also be viewed as such because of their phenotype and physical characteristics (including skin color, ethnic clothing, etc.). The contextual nature of racialization also means that Muslims, and other non-Islamic brown-skinned people are experiencing more discrimination because of their religious identity today than in the past, and arguably more so after the 2016 Presidential Election.

Furthermore, notions of "good Muslims", who denounce violent acts, do not wear veils, and sacrifice their cultural/ethnic identity, are seen as acceptable, while "bad Muslims" are viewed as radical terrorists. These stereotypes have real consequences for communities of color, refugees, and immigrants. The impact of racial/ethnic and religious profiling has resulted in discriminatory practices that target minorities while fostering distrust in law enforcement. Community surveillance, along with violations of the civil rights of Muslims in the US has fractured citizen–government relationships, which further impacts on violence, and the reporting of hate crimes, and fosters fear in communities.

The Research Evidence

While data on this phenomenon are limited, the spike in Islamophobia, and subsequent initial counting of anti-Muslim bias incidents, can be observed in the months following 9/11, as Muslim people from diverse backgrounds experienced violence and discrimination; 1,700 acts of hate violence were recorded. In 2016, 2,213 bias incidents against Muslims in the US related to religious, ethnic, or national origin were reported. These incidents occurred in residential communities (385), schools/colleges (273), and public spaces (627), thus reflecting the increasing prevalence of anti-Muslim bias (CAIR, 2017). In 2017, more than 300 Islamophobic incidents against South Asian, Muslim, Sikh, and Middle Eastern people (including refugees), which included fearmongering, mosque attacks, bullying/harassment in schools, and vandalism to homes and businesses, were documented, an increase not observed since 9/11.

Islamophobia has reshaped both Muslim American and Muslim immigrant identities and communities, while the racialization of religion has had social consequences for various racial/ethnic groups including Arab Americans, South Asians, and African Americans, exacerbating the risk of gendered violence via hypervisibility,[6] and for immigrants and refugees through racial profiling and stigmatization. Furthermore, 'mistakenly Muslim' communities, including Sikhs,[7] Hindus, and Latinos, have also been impacted by anti-Muslim sentiment in the years since 9/11.[8] Because Islamophobia links domestic and foreign policy where the state-led persecution of Muslims becomes normalized, it is also important to consider the global impact of anti-Muslim policy, surveillance, and public sentiment. For example, grassroots organizations in the US working to combat Islamophobia have argued that the War on Terror's specific targeting of people racialized as Muslim and 'other' is intended to expand global empire and ultimately, the prison nation, thus, it is important to acknowledge violence against Muslim people on a global scale.

- NYPD Muslim Surveillance Unit (2003–2014) gathered intel on Muslim communities; focused on 28 ancestries from South Asia/ Middle East, creating maps of ethnic neighborhoods; records of Muslim restaurants, mosques, businesses; Muslim students on college campuses and was criticized for violating rights of Muslim Americans and harming national security.
- National Security Entry-Exit Registration System (NSEERS) (2002– 2016) targeted Middle Eastern, Arab, South Asian Muslims; age 16+ from 25 predominantly Muslim nations and resulted in over 13,000 deportations without due process, registration, and interrogation of 80,000 men, and never resulted in any terrorism convictions.
- Law enforcement and media bias continues to skew accurate coverage of anti-Muslim crimes. For example, the murder of three University of North Carolina–Chapel Hill students in 2015 was not initially counted as an Islamophobic attack. Yusor Mohammad Abu-Salha, 21; her husband, Deah Barakat, 23; and her sister, Razan Mohammad Abu-Salha, 19, were targeted and killed; however, law enforcement initially deemed the killings as motivated by a parking dispute despite more than 100 Muslim advocacy groups calling for a federal investigation citing the rise of anti-Muslim bias.
- Executive Order 13769 (Travel Ban 2017): 700 (predominantly Muslim) travelers were detained, and up to 60,000 visas revoked.
- 2,213 anti-Muslim hate incidents in 2016, along with an increase in hate groups.
- Of 302 incidents against South Asian, Muslim, Sikh, Hindu, Middle Eastern people, women were the victims of 213 incidents, and of these, 63 percent wore the hijab (Muslim veil).

- In 2017, over half a million Rohingya Muslims were refugees from Myanmar who had crossed into Bangladesh as a result of state-based atrocities and fear of genocide.
- By 2018, over one million Uighurs had disappeared into re-education camps in China.

Recommendations and Solutions

1. Social recognition of the interconnectedness of Islamophobia with xenophobia and anti-Black racism is necessary to address social biases and the complex marginalization of minority groups.
2. In accordance with point 1, addressing the historical normalization of anti-Muslim bias before the onset of post-9/11 surveillance policies, specifically, the history of racial exclusion of South Asians, is required to address the enduring nature of discrimination in the legal system as race/ethnicity are utilized to form policy. For example, racial profiling at airports, via biased media depictions, and societal assumptions of criminality based on racial/ethnic or national identity, especially in the aftermath of mass shootings or terror-related incidents. Acknowledging how marginalized groups are excluded is necessary to address discriminatory practices that impede religious freedom and civil rights. Furthermore, it is necessary to examine the connections between Islamophobia and anti-Sikh and anti-Black/Brown violence in the United States particularly in the case of 'mistaken identity' hate crimes that stem from discrimination, stereotyping, and xenophobia.
3. Conducting intersectional research in this area (across multiple identities including gender, race, ethnicity, national origin, legal/citizen and refugee status, etc.) is critically needed to assess the impact of Islamophobia on both a national and global scale. Increased data collection can not only provide a more comprehensive understanding of anti-Muslim bias as a social issue but insight into the intersectional nature of the problem is also critical to eliminating this form of racism that also has gendered implications. Data collection beyond just Muslim ethnic-enclave communities is necessary.
4. Acknowledging U.S. Islamophobia post-9/11 as unique but, at the same time, also intertwined with global anti-Muslim bias that transgresses borders and normalizes violence against racial/ethnic and religious minorities. It is important to consider the case of refugees and state violence abroad including Rohingya Muslims, Chinese Uighurs, and state rights in both Assam and Kashmir, India.

5. Collaborative efforts with community leaders, non-profits, and governmental organizations in ways that center the voices of Muslim people but do not exploit the communities via surveillance-based policies are required. Centering Muslim-led grassroots organizations that counter multifaceted Islamophobic issues including racial profiling, international human rights violations, gender-based violence such as harassment in public spaces, and hate crimes, are all necessary to support measures that aim to prohibit religious-based discrimination. While media framing is increasingly difficult to counter, social justice organizations on the ground have organized to call attention to anti-Muslim policies.[9] However, successfully addressing and resisting normalized and state-led violence requires working with Muslim communities, cultural organizations, and non-profits to promote understanding of differences and challenge stereotypes that can address social inequality.

6. The enduring legacies of surveillance-based programs and policies against immigrants and religious minorities through the Department of Homeland Security, Immigration and Customs Enforcement and The Department of Justice needs to be acknowledged in order to examine the escalation and expansion of powers that have restricted Muslim American citizens' freedom in the United States. Specifically addressing the impact of the Travel Ban, the impact on Muslim communities in both the US and abroad, the normalization of political rhetoric tinged with xenophobic and Islamophobic sentiment that foster violence against marginalized groups, as well as the increased targeting of communities of color, requires seeking political accountability from representatives and transparency from law enforcement agencies. National governments can also be encouraged by international legislative bodies and agencies such as the United Nations to review legal policies and procedures that violate the rights of citizens, immigrants, and refugees. Furthermore, halting the expansion of CVE (Countering Violent Extremism) grants today that target specific minority communities nationally including Muslims, immigrants, refugees, and Black Lives Matter organizers, including students at schools and universities throughout the US, are important, while demanding transparency about policies that impede citizens' rights.

7. The underreporting of hate crimes motivated by racial, ethnic, or religious minority status should also be addressed via implementing culturally sensitive training for responders and adequate support for victims reporting sensitive crimes to law enforcement. Special

services for victims of immigrant and religious-based incidents may be needed especially given the history of suspicion, surveillance, and mistrust between law enforcement and marginalized communities including Muslims, immigrants, and people of color, thus changes in training protocols that reduce barriers to reporting and foster a sense of community trust are also necessary.

8. Addressing the rising fears surrounding Sharia Law that can be observed through the passage of over 200 anti-Muslim bills in the United States in recent years that portray Islamic religious law as an infiltration of international law in the US. This requires increased vigilance from researchers, activists, and representatives, to recognize and counter discriminatory bills. Furthermore, the international community can aid in this matter by reviewing laws that violate religious freedom and promote intolerance against marginalized citizens.

9. Support for inclusive intersectional diversity and respect for difference that acknowledges societal normalization of Islamophobic bias, as well as media tropes of "good" and "bad" Muslims can be addressed via social media, as well as creative social justice publicity campaigns that counter Islamophobia and dispel stereotypical narratives and display support for marginalized communities. For example, as a result of gendered Islamophobia towards elderly veiled women using public transportation, Boston launched a poster campaign encouraging bystanders to intervene in anti-Muslim incidents by sitting with victims and discussing neutral topics to deter harassment. Around the city, 50 posters of the bystander's guide to Islamophobia featuring a cartoon by Paris-based artist Maeril was implemented as a simple strategy to fight intolerance with education.

10. Finally, in educational institutions, addressing intolerance at the K-12 level by promoting inclusive school environments, teacher training related to anti-Muslim and anti-immigrant bullying, as well as diversity training related to cultural competence can aid in alleviating prejudiced behaviors that can escalate to violence and normalize Islamophobia and xenophobia. In higher education, promoting diversity training, inclusive leadership, and culturally competent counseling and reporting services can aid in documenting this understudied form of violence. Additionally, effectively implemented university policies and procedures surrounding bias against marginalized populations, including international, immigrant, racial/ethnic and religious minorities, need further support by administrative staff, faculty, and campus police.

Notes

[1] NSEERS targeted Middle Eastern, Arab, and South Asian Muslims over the age of 16 from predominantly Muslim nations and resulted in 13,000 deportations, 80,000 interrogations, and no terrorism convictions.

[2] CVE aims to deter US residents from joining violent extremist groups by bringing together community and religious leaders with law enforcement, teachers, and social service employees. It results in the stigmatization of a community as suspect.

[3] The USA Patriot Act, which was intended to detect terrorism, was criticized for allowing the invasion of citizens' privacy (indefinite detention of immigrants; law enforcement search of homes/businesses without consent; telephone, email, financial records accessed without court orders). It also resulted in increasing the powers of the National Security Agency and the US Foreign Intelligence Surveillance Court to obtain and share information on US citizens and foreigners.

[4] The NYPD Muslim Surveillance Program gathered intelligence on Muslim communities in the New York City area with a focus on 28 ancestries from South Asia and the Middle East, which included creating maps of ethnic enclave communities, keeping records of Muslim restaurants, businesses, and mosques, as well as lists of Muslims students attending college in the tri-state area. It was subsequently criticized for violating the rights of Muslim Americans and harming national security.

[5] The term "crisis of citizenship" emerges from the literature on the experiences of Arab Detroit post 9/11. National and political crises intensify debates regarding citizenship, thus ideas of citizenship making and security are also reshaped. These historical circumstances result in the general public and political actors redefining who is a citizen and who has sights as such, and in examinations of how diversity or difference is reconciled in relation to ideas of belonging and unity in a society. See Citizenship and Crisis Arab Detroit after 9/11 for further information.

[6] Women who veil are particularly vulnerable to threat and assault (Perry, 2014).

[7] For example, almost 200 hate crimes against Sikhs have occurred since 2001; a group more likely to experience discrimination as a result of misconceptions of Muslim appearance and biases, yet many of these incidents go unreported or accurate data is not collected (The Sikh Coalition, 2018).

[8] Documented incidents of 'mistaken identity' Islamophobic violence towards Hindus (predominantly Indian and Indian Americans), Latinos, West Indians, and other marginalized communities that are racially profiled as Muslim. There have been 175+ anti-Sikh hate crimes since 9/11 including the Oak Creek massacre; Sikhs are hundreds of times more likely to experience hate crimes in the US because of their distinct appearance that includes wearing turbans and long beards that have been associated with the Taliban through U.S. media images. Violence against Sikhs go unreported, and government officials have neglected to collect accurate data about the problem.

[9] This includes addressing organizational awareness and training that inform racial profiling and biases as documented with The Sikh Coalition's *Ending TSA Profiling* initiative.

Key Resources

Ayoub, A., & Beydoun, K. (2017). Executive Disorder: The Muslim Ban, Emergency Advocacy, and the Fires Next Time. *Michigan Journal of Race and Law,* 22(2), 215–241.

Beydoun, K. (2018). *American Islamophobia: Understanding the roots and rise of fear.* Oakland, California: University of California Press.

Detroit Arab American Study Team (2009). *Citizenship and crisis: Arab Detroit after 9/11.* New York: Russell Sage Foundation.

Kumar, D. (2012). *Islamophobia and the politics of empire.* Chicago, Illinois: Haymarket Press.

Love, E. (2017). *Islamophobia and racism in America.* New York: New York University Press.

Mir, S. (2014). *Muslim American women on campus: Undergraduate social life and identity.* Chapel Hill, NC: UNC Press.

Perry, B. (2014). Gendered Islamophobia: Hate crimes against Muslim women. *Social Identities,* 20(1), 74–89.

Raja, D. (2019) Almost twenty years later: Lessons learned from critical resistance and INCITE! on building an organizing framework to tackle violence at the nexus of state violence, gender-based violence, and structural islamophobia. *WSQ: Women's Studies Quarterly,* 47(3–4), 276–282.

Selod, S. (2018). *Forever suspect: Racialized surveillance of Muslim Americans in the War on Terror.* New Brunswick: Rutgers University Press.

Selod, S. (2016). The politics of Islamophobia: Race, power and fantasy. *Sociology of Race and Ethnicity,* 2(1), 120–121.

Singh, J. (2013). A new American apartheid: Racialized, religious minorities in the post-9/11 era. *Sikh Formations,* 9(2), 115–144.

South Asian Americans Leading Together (SAALT) (2018). *Communities on Fire: Confronting Hate Violence and Xenophobic Political Rhetoric.* Retrieved from http://saalt.org/report communities-on-fire-confronting-hate-violence-and-xenophobic-political-rhetoric/

TWO

Latinos are Each of Us: Fair and Just Immigration Policies for All

Noreen M. Sugrue and Sylvia Puente

Fair and just policies centering on immigrants and immigrations must reflect the data as well as values and ideals of words inscribed on the Statue of Liberty:

> Give me your tired, your poor, Your huddled masses yearning to breathe free, The wretched refuse of your teeming shore. Send these, the homeless, tempest-tost to me, I lift my lamp beside the golden door!

The Problem

According to the President, many members of Congress, numerous state and local officials, and an embarrassingly large percentage of the general public, Latinos are immigrants and just do not belong here. These views and beliefs persist in spite of the fact that in 2017, there were about 56.8 million Latinos in the US, 19.7 million or 34 percent of whom were immigrants, leaving 39.1 million or just under two thirds of whom were U.S. citizens.

Current immigration policies, ICE raids, and deportation activities, as well as the descriptions of Latinos coming to or currently living in the US, would lead one to believe that most Latinos in this country are foreigners, very few are citizens, and they do not contribute to the social good. In fact, they are too often described as being a social problem, exacerbating violence, ruining communities, taking handouts, and contributing little, if anything, to the social, political, and economic stability and health of the US. Public policies increasingly are reflecting this distorted, inaccurate, and hateful discourse. That is, public policies continue to take aim at Latinos as if they are out to destroy the US economy and way of way life by eroding the country's social and cultural DNA. The reality is that Latinos, like every other immigrant group past and present, be they asylum seekers, documented immigrants, undocumented immigrants, naturalized citizens, or native born, are making significant and essential contributions to the well-being of all residing in the US.

The Research Evidence

We cannot ignore that it is the hateful bigotry that seems to be the foundation for far too many discussions and policy decisions regarding immigration and immigrants generally, and Latinos specifically. Therefore, we turn to facts about who Latinos are and what they are contributing to the US, all with the intent of providing a foundation of truth in order to better explore fairer and just social policies for immigration, all immigrants, and each of us living in the US.

Today, more than 321 million people live in the US; slightly more than 44 million are immigrants, making immigrants about 14 percent of the total US population. In 2000, approximately 40 percent of Latinos were foreign born; today, according to Pew Research, about 34 percent are foreign born. There are over 56 million Latinos living in the US which translates into almost 18 percent of the US population being Latino; that percentage will only continue to grow for the foreseeable future.

A common ugly untrue charge that is far too often leveled against all Latinos, especially the undocumented, and is used as a justification for public policies such as the change in the definition of public charge, is that Latinos are taking advantage of the system and "getting all kinds of government support and free stuff" paid for by hardworking "real" Americans. One way to document that this charge is false is to examine labor force and economic data.

According to the Bureau of Labor Statistic (BLS), in 2017, the labor force participation rate for Latinos was 66.1 percent, regardless of country of origin, while the rate for non-Latinos was 62.2 percent.

According to other reports, another way to understand the economic contributions of Latinos in the US is: If U.S. Latinos were their own nation, they would have the world's seventh-largest gross domestic product (GDP), at $2.13 trillion. According to a research center at the University of Georgia, this year Latino purchasing power will top $1.7 billion.

Finally, in 2019 earning an income that was 200 percent of the federal poverty level translated into an annual salary of $24,980 for one person or $51,500 for a family of four. Forty percent of undocumented workers earn at or above 200 percent of the federal poverty level. This means that even if they were legally entitled to apply for government benefits and subsidies, which they are not, their incomes would make them ineligible; simply put, they earn too much.

It is commonly noted, or at least implied, that only Latinos are undocumented. Another claim we hear all too often is that undocumented Latinos are poor, they are now crossing the border in the largest numbers ever to do bad things, and they are using U.S.-born children for "chain migration". All of these charges are untrue.

And, while it is true that Latinos are a significant share of undocumented workers, their numbers have been dropping since 2008. At the same time, significantly measurable numbers of undocumented workers from other parts of world are living in the US (e.g., 16 percent are from Asia and 13 percent are from every other region in the world, including Europe, Canada, and Africa).

Robert Sampson, a sociologist at Harvard points out that communities with high numbers of Latino immigrants, regardless of status, have far lower rates of crime than similar communities that are dominate by native-born people.

It should also be noted that undocumented Latinos in the US, far from recently arriving to get "free stuff from the government" or having children here to function as "anchor babies", are long term working age residents who have high rates of employment. Specifically, 62 percent have been in the US for more than 10 years and 21 percent have been living in the US for more than 20 years. Of the 66 percent who are between the ages of 25 and 54, 67 percent of this group are employed, compared to only 58 percent of the US born in the same age group.

Another untrue charge that drives unjust and unfair policies is that undocumented Latino immigrants are almost all males who speak no English and live in horrible conditions that are detrimental to neighborhoods. Almost half (47 percent) of undocumented immigrants are female and only about 44 percent of the undocumented speak no English or do not speak it very well. At the same time, almost 10 percent of undocumented Latinos speak only English and 34 percent of them own their own home.

Latino immigrants and their American children are the catalyst for creating immigration reform. And those reforms must be framed in terms of social justice, fairness, and equity. In other words, immigration policies must not reflect the misrepresentations, fear peddling, vilifications, and lies currently perpetuated by words and the misuse of data.

Addressing the language used in public discourse is necessary but difficult. How we speak of something or someone reveals our values and underlying views; it shapes how we define problems and structure solutions. Too much of today's discourse surrounding immigration and immigrants gives rise to policies that are unfair and unjust, to say the least. While language use cannot be legislated, every one of us has the moral responsibility to counter and challenge all distortions, lies, and attacks that are verbally hoisted onto immigrants. Each of us must speak truth to power and hate. It is when that occurs that we have the best chance of designing and implementing fair and just social policies.

Recommendations and Solutions

Policies related to immigration and immigrants must be built on two principles. The first is that immigration reforms and policies should be tied to the economic and social needs of the US, most notably economic growth and development. There is no disputing that immigration is a necessary condition for the US to secure both economic and population growth. Without growth in those two areas, the long-term stability and security of the country is not guaranteed. The second principle is the US's humanitarian and moral responsibilities to those seeking opportunity, safety, and protection; the US has a moral duty to these people. The US has these duties and obligations because of its power, wealth, and history. It is a national noblesse oblige.

Policy solutions are not easy. Immigration is complicated but if approached from the framework of social justice and fairness, there are many options available to states and the federal government. However, before embracing specific solutions, it must be underscored that the first step in addressing anything related to immigration or any immigrant is that all discussions and proposed solutions and policies must be grounded in the data. Further, the lies and vitriolic disdain for immigrants that all too often dominate the public discourse today must stop. It is a truism to note that without a change in that discourse there will be no policy changes because the two are inexorably linked. Truth, facts, and fairness must be what shape our words so that our policies also can be shaped within the same context.

Although the data here are primarily Latino based, it is important to remember that immigration policies are written for all immigrants. The horrific treatment targeted at and vicious attacks on Latinos coming, or who have come, to the US through the southern border are driving the need for policy changes and recommendations that will restructure how immigrants are treated. These policy changes are required in order to redress the unspeakably immoral treatment of Latino immigrants as well as their U.S. families. Latinos have borne an unconscionable amount of abuse and discrimination; rectifying those through improving immigration policies will benefit all immigrants and all native-born Americans. And, such reforms and policies will go a long way in ensuring that each of us lives not in a perfect union, but rather in a country that continually strives to be a more perfect union.

The following are specific policy recommendations that should be instituted immediately because they are just. In addition, these policy proposals will benefit the nation and all living within its borders, regardless of where they or their ancestors were born.

1. All Immigration and Customs Enforcements (ICE) raids must stop for at least four years.
   There are two exceptions to this:
   i. National security risks, which must be demonstrated to a judicial panel of three federal judges. All evidence presented for such cases must meet the criminal standards of collection, chain of command, and constitutional protections for alleged criminals.
   ii. Conviction of violent criminal offense. Any convictions used as a basis for deportation must have exhausted the constitutionally guaranteed appellate processes, which are open to all who come before the criminal justice system.
2. There must be an allocation of whatever money and resources are required in order to guarantee adequate numbers of appropriately trained staff so that there is a timely processing of applications for all who are seeking entry into the US.
   i. There needs to be a determination of specifically how much time is required for the "timely processing of applications for all seeking entry into the US".
3. The number of immigration judges must be increased to meet the demand for fair and just processing of all applications.
4. There must be a fair and reasonably easy path to citizenship for all undocumented immigrants who have not met the exception to deportations criteria.
5. All money for the erection of a border wall must be frozen for five years. This will provide enough time for fair and just immigration policies to be enacted. In addition, it will provide a short-term period for the evaluation of how these policies are working and living up to the two principles that guided their development and implementation.
6. Any legal challenges to the policies suggested here, or any other policy initiatives that meet the two principles laid out earlier, must be given expedited hearings and reviews in the courts.

7. All detention centers, camps, or holding facilities of any kind must be dismantled immediately.
8. There will be no family separation. This policy will be disbanded and legislation must be enacted to ensure such horrors can never again occur.
9. There must be both the personnel and monetary resources necessary to reunite separated families immediately.
    i. The necessary medical and mental health needs of these separated families will be met and costs will be absorbed by the federal government.
    ii. Any adoption of children separated from families at the border will be null and void. Those children will be reunited with their family in the US.
    iii. How children that are not reunited with families will be cared for will be determined not by a government agency but rather by groups put together by an array of experts in the areas of trauma, family, and abandonment. These groups will be constituted and monitored by the American Academy of Pediatrics and any other non-governmental agencies with the requisite expertise in addressing and mitigating the horrors and traumas associated with family separation.
10. We must reaffirm and ensure that we provide the constitutional guarantees that are, or should be, afforded anyone, regardless of immigration status, in the US who are confronting legal structures or institutions. In addition, there must be the creation and formalization of processes for application, review, adjudication, and appeal of request for entry into the US. And these processes must be afforded to all who seek entry, regardless of whether they enter the country by land, air, or sea. Further, those processes must differentiate between immigrants, refugees, and asylum seekers. Each of these categories carries special circumstances and needs to be treated as a sui generis category.
    i. This approach to those seeking entry into the US will ensure fairness and due process while also building trust in the system. Those three components are necessary especially since some cases will be denied.
11. There should be no laws, orders, or policies that in any way intimidate, call into question, or drive underground immigrants who live with family members who are U.S. citizens. In the case of Latinos, because this community is really a community of U.S. citizens and immigrants, all policies targeting immigrants or any family members must reflect and respect this reality.

12. Those who are residing in the US, regardless of status, require a path to stability and security. As the data document, the contributions of immigrants, regardless of status, are enormous. Those contributions must be acknowledged. Public policies must be a set of incentives for supporting the continuation of such contributions.

13. Currently, public support for immigrants is both restricted and dependent upon where immigrants and their families live. The goal is to have immigrants integrate into U.S. life – be vital and contributing members of communities, states, and the nation. If that goal is to be met, then public policies need to reflect that sometimes people need a safety net to succeed. There should be no time constraints or conditions on assisting people with food, housing, health care, transportation, language acquisition, or educational needs. This assistance should be seen as investment in the human capital and capacity that will benefit all who live in the US, regardless of where they or their parents were born.

   i. Safety net policies that are accessible with no artificial time barriers are squarely on top of the two foundational components for fair and just immigration policies.

Immigration is here to stay; immigrants, although there has been a discernible decline in numbers, will continue to come to the US. It is, therefore, incumbent upon each of us to ensure that our immigration policies are fair and just. These issues are complex, morally challenging, and any public action or response must be grounded in the realities of who immigrants are and why they immigrate, not stereotypes, purposeful lies, fear mongering, or misinformed emotional hyperbole.

Every sovereign nation has a right to control its own borders and set immigration policies. At the same time, the US and 47 other countries are signatories to the 1948 Universal Declaration of Human Rights, which notes that people have a right to migrate. This means the US, up to this point, believed that every human being had a right to move, seek shelter or refuge, but also that no nation was obligated to take all who came to and/or through their borders. Assuming each nation addresses requests for immigration, shelter, or asylum in a fair and even-handed manner, there would be trust in the process. Nations adhering to such processes become beacons and standard bearers for how to work with people moving from one nation to another. And it is with that in mind as well as a commitment to data-driven social-justice-oriented policies that a fair, humane, and workable immigration system is possible in the US. Such a system benefits the society overall as well as the immigrants and their descendants, and that is what is fair and just in a democracy.

Key Resources

Davis, Julie Hirschfeld and Michael D. Shear. 2019. *Border Wars: Inside Trump's Assault on Immigration*. New York: Simon and Schuster.

DeParle, Jason. 2019. *A Good Provider is One Who Leaves: One Family and Immigration in the 21st Century*. New York: Penguin Random House.

Hendricks, Kasey, et al. 2017. *A Tale of Three Cities: The State of Racial Justice in Chicago*. Chicago: Institute for Research on Race and Public Policy, University of Illinois at Chicago. Retrieved July 7, 2019. (https://stateofracialjusticechicago.com/a-tale-of-three-cities).

McDermott, Monica. 2006. *Working Class Whites: The Making and Unmaking of Race Relations*. Berkeley: University of California Press.

Noe-Bustanmante, Luisard and Antonio Flores. 2019. *Facts on Latinos in the U.S.* Washington D.C.: Pew Research Center Hispanic Trends. Retrieved September 20, 2019. (https://www.pewresearch.org/hispanic/fact-sheet/latinos-in-the-u-s-fact-sheet/).

Sandoval-Strausz, A.K. 2019. *Barrio America: How Latino Immigrants Saved the American City*. New York: Basic Books.

Sawhill, Isabel. 2018. *The Forgotten Americans: An Economic Agenda for a Divided Nation*. New Haven: Yale University Press.

Shapiro, Thomas M. 2017. *Toxic Inequality: How America's Wealth Gap Destroys Mobility, Deepens the Racial Divide, and Threatens Our Future*. New York: Basic Books.

Vissek, M. Anne and Edwin Melendez. 2015. "Working in the New Low Wage Economy: Understanding Participation in Low-Wage Employment in the Recessionary Era." *The Journal of Labor and Society*, 18: 7–29.

Zepeds-Millan, Chris. 2017. *Latino Mass Mobilization: Immigration, Racialization, and Activism*. Cambridge: Cambridge University Press.

THREE

The Intersection of Gender and Race in U.S. Family Law: Persistent Social Inequities and Rollback Reforms

Bronwen Lichtenstein

The Problem

Family law in the United States is contested terrain, subject to the push-pull of history, gender wars, racial bias (think "Welfare Queen"), and social change. In the 1970s, no-fault divorce law was deemed revolutionary for the times. With the promise of a less adversarial, expensive, and contrived end to marriage, couples no longer had to prove misconduct such as adultery, neglect, or domestic violence in order to divorce or to claim child custody and fair division of the marital property. Social progressives hailed this change as a victory for gender equity, but critiques of no-fault divorce law began almost immediately. Two examples go to the crux of the matter. First, with fewer assets than men, women often received less in "equitable" settlements (a standard used by the court). Second, the court interpreted equity as a level playing field without regard to structural inequalities at home and in the workplace. To quote family law icon, the late Herma Hill Kay,

> The no-fault divorce law [posited] that men and women should be treated as equals under the law. In the seventeen years that witnessed those fundamental changes, judicial implementation of the combined philosophies of no-fault divorce and equality between women and men proved inadequate in the context of financial settlements following marital dissolution [...] Women and children have borne the brunt of the transition [and] further changes are required to prevent such unfortunate and unnecessary results.

Family law scholars argue no-fault divorce contributes to gender inequality in three specific ways. First, women who seek alimony are framed as dependent, even parasitic, on ex-husbands. Second, children are the focus of competing claims under the equity rule. Three, fewer mothers receive custody despite women's roles as caregivers during marriage.

Family law also took a revolutionary turn when, in 1996, the state sought to reduce welfare rolls by collecting and enforcing child support payments. In this role, officials ensured fathers (for the most part) met their financial obligations to support dependent children. In the wake of this reform, income transfers from non-custodial to custodial parents aligned more closely to traditional child support, a pattern that continued until state enforcement procedures were challenged in a case that came before the U.S. Supreme Court. The 2011 verdict was a victory for indigent fathers because the court ruled petitions for child support arrears must include evidence of the obligor's ability to pay. The outcome for low-income women and children, especially in communities of color, is less access to state enforcement of child support arrears.

This chapter argues women have lost ground in rollback reforms that stratify by race and class in modern society. In 2018, the U.S. Institute for Policy Studies reported a widening gap in gender-based inequality over the past 50 years, a finding relevant to procedures in family law and policy described in this chapter. The gap shows up in race-wealth inequities disproportionately affecting women of color. As reported by the Institute, Black women earn 34.2 percent less than White men; they also earn less than Black men and all other workers. The chapter will describe some important changes affecting women across the sociocultural spectrum, and call for policies to prevent further erosion of income parity. I will present four solutions to address the gendered, raced, and often invisible effects of these reforms in U.S. family law and policy.

The Research Evidence

There are two main research areas of family law and policy. The first area examines the rights, obligations, and outcomes of divorcing couples. These families are often better off (and Whiter) than their non-married counterparts. The second area looks at custody, visitation, and support of children in non-traditional families, often in communities of color. Compared to divorce, whose rates have declined in recent years, a growing number of children (one-third of the U.S. total), live in non-traditional families. Gender-race inequities arise at these intersections of family law and policy.

Divorce

Is divorce an equalizing process? Sociologists Karen Holden and Pamela Smock say no. In their 1991 systematic review of research on post-divorce income in the *Annual Review of Sociology,* the authors gave ample evidence of how men's incomes rose in comparison to the trajectory of "prolonged and negative" financial hardships for women. Estimates vary as to the level of difference, but scholars from the United States and further afield agree the gender gap is significant in post-divorce and likely to persist over the life course. Despite its early promise, no-fault divorce contributes to this gendered outcome. To illustrate, Lichtenstein and Johnson's 2018 article on property division in the *Journal of Divorce & Remarriage* showed most filers were women (70 percent) who petitioned for ownership of the property. Despite this preference, their husbands took possession of the marital property two-thirds of the time, either by court order or buying out the woman's share. This gain meant post-divorce wealth accrued to the men through property acquisition and the equity it builds. The court also applied the "higher-income" principle in their dispositions, which typically favored men. The authors showed hiring an attorney benefitted men's claims as well, with 83 percent of husbands acquiring the marital property at settlement. Although some jurisdictions have different rules, children did not factor into these decisions in the study locale, and custodial parents did not have the upper hand when they petitioned for the marital home.

Other flashpoints for gender equality involve money and children. Rules for spousal maintenance and child custody could favor women in the days before the no-fault divorce revolution, especially if they were deemed the "innocent party" because of husbands' philandering. In the no-fault law era, spousal maintenance (alimony) suffers the common perception of wives "taking men to the cleaners" (legal analyses dispute this claim), of ridicule when spousal payments extend to men, and of political pressure to strike it from the books. A Florida bill sought to do just that when reformers sought to end permanent awards in the 2019 legislative session, and promised further action in 2020. However, alimony is already rare in the United States. As reported by legal scholars Judith McMullen and Debra Oswald in the 2011 issue of *Marquette Law Scholarly Commons*, judges award alimony about 8 percent of the time (an historical low), with most payments ending after a few years.

The judicial retreat from alimony obscures the reality of married women who spend lengthy periods away from the workforce for child-rearing and domestic duties. Such women often lack skills for reentry, face age discrimination from employers, and experience financial hardship in post-divorce and beyond. The end of alimony, as commonly predicted, also parallels the end of the "maternal preference" standard in awarding custody in fault-based divorces. In the no-fault divorce era, "best interests of the child" is the gender-neutral, *de jure* basis for deciding custody. In research published in *Family Law Quarterly* titled "Are mothers losing custody?" Mary Ann Mason and Ann Quirk show men equally likely to win child custody disputes in the no-fault era, despite women's greater contribution to caregiving during marriage. This paradox has prompted calls from family law scholars and others to revamp judicial decision-making for child custody provisions in the United States.

Child Support

In 1996, the Personal Responsibility and Work Opportunity Reconciliation Act (PRWORA) revolutionized the structure of the U.S. social safety net. Among a slew of welfare-to-work reforms, President Bill Clinton's promise of "the most sweeping crackdown on deadbeat parents in history" promoted strict enforcement of child support orders. The state hardened its approach to non-payers by garnishing their wages, tracking them across state lines, taking away their driver's licenses and, when all else failed, incarcerating them. Lynne Haney's 2018 article about incarcerated fathers in *American Journal of Sociology* documented how poor men (often African Americans) were locked up in record numbers for failure to pay child support, and locked up again when they failed to pay arrears during their prison sentence. A 2009 report by the Urban Institute showed 70 percent of arrears attributable to under- or unemployed fathers.

The practice of incarcerating (mostly) poor men ended when the U.S. Supreme Court ruled evidence of a defendant's ability to pay child support must be established in civil contempt cases, a task requiring formal documentation of all sources of income. In a lateral if not related development, cuts to federal funding for arrears enforcement occurred after 2016. Some states responded to *Turner* and the cuts by curtailing their legal support role (or through triage), leaving custodial mothers few options for relief unless they could afford an attorney. Research on the impact of the *Turner* rule has yet to emerge beyond a few reports of smaller caseloads and judicial hearings for child support arrears. Elizabeth Patterson's 2017 study titled "Turner in the Trenches," found a measurable decline in arrears petitions after the rule came into effect in South Carolina. Lichtenstein's (2019) study found a 30 percent drop in petitions in the year after *Turner* operationalized in Alabama. In the latter case, 82 percent of post-*Turner* petitioners were women who filed their own claims for enforcement, with Black women making up two-thirds of the total. For the most part, these petitions failed because, without state support, the plaintiffs walked away or, if they proceeded, lost their case. In other dismissals, the non-payers had disappeared or died, were ill, disabled, or serving time for other crimes, or the minor child had turned 19 and no longer qualified for child support. In the small number of cases with a verdict, the non-payers typically received a suspended sentence rather than jail. Although the state has restored a measure of support for "provable" cases after a flurry of complaints from the judiciary, the number of petitions continues to fall, and these often end in dismissal.

Recommendations and Solutions

These rollback reforms signal a troubled landscape for gender justice in family law. At one end of the income scale, alimony is deemed anachronistic, a perk for the idle rich, and unfair to men who want to get on with their lives. Lost in this reframing is the persistent gender inequity that widens after divorce. At the other end of the scale, cutbacks to child support enforcement harm poor mothers who do not own property, receive alimony, or have other sources of wealth to ensure their family's well-being. This march to poverty has gathered pace despite the list of "must do's" in The Child Support Enforcement Act of 1984, and stands to accelerate further after proposed cuts to food stamps for low-income families in the Trump era. Word is likely to spread to non-custodial parents who lack verifiable income that they no longer need to fear the enforcement apparatus of the state; the effects on custodial parents and children are yet to be measured in terms of cumulative disadvantage. Under current conditions, women and children are likely to be poorer, gender-race divisions are likely to intensify, and social distress will spread further than documented by the U.S. Institute of Policy Studies. In scaling back its enforcement role, the state fails to seek middle ground between locking up indigent fathers and protecting children from poverty. Taken together, these policy reversals undercut the ideal of reducing the gender gap in wealth equity, and signal an end to the progressive era.

Solutions are needed to address these changes in family law and policy, and to counter powerful social forces inhibiting women's progress toward equality. I make the following four recommendations for reductions in gender conflict over custody and assets, and for restoring the once firmly held idea that women and children should not be impoverished after relationship dissolution or divorce.

1. Adopt American Law Institute Policies to End Conflict over Child Custody, Child Support, and Alimony

Before her death in 2017, Herma Hill Kay urged adoption of the American Law Institute's "Principles of the Law of Family Dissolution" in order to reduce power struggles over child custody, visitation, child support, and alimony. This recommendation should be implemented to ensure fairer outcomes in divorce settlements. Chapter Two of the "Principles," which covers these matters, sets out a formula whereby the division of (caregiving) labor during marriage is used to determine which parent gets primary custody, termed "the approximation standard." The standard takes parenting ability and quality of emotional attachment into account, and removes the perverse incentive of using custody as a bargaining chip for gaining the lion's share of marital assets and/or possession of the family home. Legal justification for the change is threefold. First, fathers' threats of protracted custody fights (a tactic Kay and others described as "extortionate") seek to convince mothers to accept less alimony and child support in exchange for primary custody. Second, in a victory for men's rights, non-custodial fathers gained greater control over family decisions by way of joint legal custody, despite women providing most of the physical and emotional labor for children after divorce. Third, custody has been used for leverage in gaining the marital home, but not in expected direction (i.e., to protect mothers and children from precarious housing). Adopting the approximation standard would help to balance the equity stakes during and after divorce.

2. Provide a 50/50 Split for Property Division

The marital home is an important asset, often split equally in community-standard jurisdictions. An important step toward gender parity would be to adopt the 50/50 split for marital property as guaranteed in the community-standard states of Arizona, California, Idaho, Louisiana, Nevada, New Mexico, Texas, Washington, and Wisconsin. The remaining states divide the marital home and assets on an equitable basis if couples cannot decide for themselves. For the court, "equitable" is a fairness standard to determine the couple's respective financial contributions during marriage and, where relevant, which party is in the best financial position to service a mortgage. Divorce lawyers describe it as vague, inconsistent, and subjective; researchers describe it as unfair to the financially weaker party. The standard is thus inequitable in practice.

Partial remedies are available even if states do not adopt the 50/50 rule. Job stability can be used to offset the higher income standard for splitting the marital home. Although women generally earn less compared to men, especially after having children, their clustering in education, nursing, retail, and office administration offers greater job security than male-dominated fields such as construction, trucking, mining, and manufacturing, which are prone to layoffs. The "best interests of the child" standard could also apply to property division, as happens in many (but not all) states, where custodial parents live in the family home until children are 18 years old. Broader adoption of this rule would result in fewer divorced women moving to less desirable housing and neighborhoods, and less disruption for children removed from their homes, schools, and family and community networks when the family divides.

3. Close the Gender–Wealth Gap through Equitable Alimony

The legal rationale for alimony is to compensate for unequal gender roles in marriage. This notion is deemed archaic, even extortionate in the modern era, but the gender–wealth gap tells a different story. A 2018 Bureau of Statistics' report showed fewer than half (46 percent) of adult women working full time, which can lead to financial hardship after separation or divorce. Women's workforce participation has not equalized as predicted by no-fault divorce reformers of the civil rights era. The court should therefore take financial disparities into account in deciding how marital assets are divided when women's roles (still traditional in many areas of the country) are defined by caregiving and part-time or supplemental employment. Although alimony is not a perfect tool for gender justice, particularly for women who do not marry, or who lack property and assets to divide in divorce, the wealth gap should not be used to justify an end to spousal support. Inequities are resolved only by challenging the often invisible hand women are played in family law and backlash reforms serving to whittle away women's rights.

4. Restore Full State Oversight of Child Support Enforcement

A critical step in meeting the "best interests of the child" standard as espoused by official, political, and legal entities is to restore funding for timely and reasonable arrears enforcement, which means finding a balance between the obligor's ability to pay and financial support for children. Relatedly, cases should not drag on for years or until the statute of limitations runs out. If state actors view these recommendations as too onerous or costly because of funding cutbacks and/or due process requirements, then the burden of proof will transfer to women. A second step is to provide job services for poor fathers in order to promote employability and their financial means to pay child support. This idea has received wholesale support from some states (e.g., Texas), some legislators, and members of the public concerned about the social impact of *Turner*, but a job plan was notably absent from the Final Rule. Revisiting this idea would follow the 2016 Federal Register's' recommendation for further study, pending action. A third step is for social scientists to examine the real-world effects of *Turner* beyond snapshots of jurisdictions that balked at implementation. Policymakers will remain unaware of the true impact of *Turner* and its sequelae until a comprehensive assessment is conducted at the national level. Finally, and more immediately, the news and social media could serve the public interest by documenting the stealth revolution in rollback reforms, the gender-class-race impacts of these changes, and the social costs of regressive politics in the current age.

The matters addressed by U.S. family law are more wide-ranging than those covered in this chapter, which has addressed two aspects of family law as experienced by women across the economic spectrum. The body of family law – pension splitting and taxation reforms included – requires constant vigilance to ensure gender-based social justice. Ideally, these laws and policies would undergo regular review in order to prevent further erosion of hard-won victories for gender equity in the United States. This chapter calls for urgent attention to widening gender-race inequalities in family law and for creative solutions to gender troubles as a social issue worthy of revolutionary change in modern society.

Key Resources

Print Resources

Kay, Herma Hill. 2002. "No-Fault Divorce and Child Custody: Chilling out the Gender Wars." *Family Law Quarterly* 36(1): 27–47.

Kisthardt, Mary Kay. 2008. "Re-Thinking Alimony: The AAML's Considerations for Calculating Alimony, Spousal Support, or Maintenance." *Journal of the Academy of Matrimonial Lawyers* 21(1): 61–85.

Leopold, Thomas. 2018. "Gender Differences in the Consequences of Divorce: A Study of Multiple Outcomes." *Demography* 55(3): 759–97.

Pedulla, David S., and Sarah Thébaud. 2015. "Can We Finish the Revolution? Gender, Work-Family Ideals and Institutional Constraint." *American Sociological Review* 80(1): 116–39.

Web Resources

Crall, Timothy. 2016. *Custodial Mothers and Fathers and Their Child Support: 2013.* Washington, DC: U.S. Census Bureau. Retrieved February 6, 2019 (https://www. census. gov/content/dam/Census/library/publications/2016/demo/P60-255.pdf).

Jenkins, Stephen P. (2008). *Marital Splits and Income Changes over the Longer Term.* Institute For Social & Economic Research. Essex University, UK. Retrieved November 9, 2017 (https://www.iser.essex.ac.uk/files/iser_working_papers/2008-07.pdf).

National Conference of State Legislatures. 2018. *Child Support and Incarceration.* Retrieved February 6, 2019 (http://www.ncsl.org/research/human-services/child-support-and- incarceration.aspx).

Sorensen, Elaine, Liliana Sousa, and Simone G. Schaner. 2007. *Assessing Child Support Arrears in Nine Large States and the Nation.* U.S. Department of Health and Human Services. Washington, DC. Retrieved February 2, 2019 (https://www.urban.org/sites/default/files/publication/29736/1001242-Assessing-Child-Support-Arrears-in-Nine- Large-States-and-the-Nation.PDF).

U.S. Federal Register. 2016. *Flexibility, Efficiency, and Modernization in Child Support Enforcement Programs.* National Archives. Washington, DC. Retrieved February 1, 2019 (https://www.federalregister.gov/documents/2016/12/20/2016–29598/flexibility-efficiency-and-modernization-in-child-support-enforcement-programs).

U.S. Supreme Court. *Turner v. Rogers, et al.,* 564 U.S. 431 (2011). Washington, DC. Retrieved February 3, 2019 (https://supreme.justia.com/cases/federal/us/564/431/).

SECTION II

Health and Families

FOUR

Reproductive Rights

Sujatha A. Jesudason

The Problem

The issues of reproductive health and rights in the United States are both confusing and contested. Some definitions of reproductive health focus only on reducing unintended pregnancies while others, according to the National Institute of Environmental Health Science, include the diseases, disorders, and conditions that affect the functioning of the *male and female* reproductive systems during *all stages of life*. In addition, there is a deeply polarizing discussion over abortion that is the result of a decades-long campaign by political conservatives. In this debate, the cultural and political understanding of reproductive health has been reduced to a moral and religious fight over abortion and the status of the fetus. This has resulted in reduced access to abortion and contraceptive services as well as limited sexuality education.

Because of this political contestation, reproductive health has become a gendered issue that is almost exclusively focused on limiting the bodily autonomy and self-determination of women and girls. Reproductive rights, reduced to a debate on the morality of abortion and when human life begins, has become a proxy contest about the role of women in political, social, and economic life, bolstered by underlying nationalist, economic, and racial anxieties.

Anti-abortion advocacy, fueled by conservative and Evangelical Christian activism, is radically committed to overturning *Roe v. Wade,* the Supreme Court ruling that legalized abortion in 1973. This promise to end legal access to abortion has driven a tidal wave of anti-abortion legislation at the state level and helped to vote Donald Trump and Mike Pence into the White House with the assurance of nominating anti-choice judges to the Supreme Court. Since 1973 these activists have passed 1,296 laws restricting access to abortion, including 278 in the last five years. Currently, 29 states are actively hostile to abortion access, and only 14 states are supportive. According to the Guttmacher

Institute, in 2019, 40 million women of reproductive age (58 percent) live in states that are hostile to abortion access.

In contrast to the pro-life movement with its singular focus on abortion, the reproductive rights movement has been a relatively fractured movement with three distinct approaches: reproductive health, reproductive rights, and reproductive justice. These different perspectives have led to a diversification of strategies that have reduced the effectiveness of the movement until recently.

The reproductive *health* sector of the movement, rooted in a public health framework of prevention, research, and health services, focuses primarily on the prevention of unintended pregnancies and sexually transmitted diseases.

The mainstream reproductive *rights* arm of the movement, primarily concerned with law and public policies, frames these concerns around legal rights and protection, and until recently, on maintaining the constitutionally protected legal right to abortion.

Reproductive *justice*, a framework articulated roughly 25 years ago by a group of Black women activists, focuses on addressing reproductive oppression experienced by historically marginalized groups and centers on an intersectional analysis of inequality. Rooted in a recognition and analysis of the long and ugly history of the rape, exploitation, control, and commodification of women of color and their children in the United States, these advocates organize for the rights of all people to have children, to not have children, and to raise those children with dignity in a healthy and safe environment.

Reproductive health advocates focus predominantly on data collection and improving health services and access. Reproductive rights advocates utilize public policy and lobbying tactics, and reproductive justice organizers primarily focus on community engagement and empowerment. These three different approaches have resulted in a rich ecology of organizations, advocates, and activists with different strategies and tactics that at times lack a unified focus. In addition, as abortion is framed as a feminist issue of gendered concern only to women, men's reproductive lives have been made invisible, inhibiting their active participation in a movement that is also about their right to have and raise healthy and safe children.

This fragmentation within the reproductive rights movement has been a legacy of the promotion of contraception, abortion, and family planning to address racialized concerns about the "overpopulation" of poor people and people of color and the advocacy of a now out-of-favor eugenics agenda. Margaret Sanger, one of the early public proponents of family planning, allied her cause with eugenicists who were interested in reducing the birth of the poor, "unfit," and people of color. Reproductive justice activists have pushed for a more inclusive, gender justice-oriented agenda that also includes the freedom to have and raise children, and not just access to abortion and contraception in order to not have children.

The Research Evidence

Based on the National Health Statistics Reports, of the 61 million women of reproductive age (15–44) in the United States, about 70 percent are sexually active but do not want to get pregnant. The vast majority of these women (99 percent) have used at least one contraceptive method at some point in their lives, with some 60 percent currently using a contraceptive method. Of the women at risk of unintended pregnancy, 10 percent don't use any contraceptive method. Nearly 45 percent of all pregnancies in the U.S. are unintended, and nearly two-fifths of those pregnancies were terminated by abortion. By the age of 45, nearly a quarter (23.7 percent) of women will have had an abortion, and 61 percent of those women will already be mothers when they have an abortion.

In terms of sexuality education, most young people aged 15–19 (80 percent) receive some formal instruction about abstinence and STD prevention. However, only 60 percent of young women and 55 percent of young men learn about birth control and pregnancy prevention methods. Increasingly, sexuality education is happening outside of the formal educational system, with less than 50 percent of high schools and 20 percent of middle schools providing comprehensive sex education, according to the National Center for HIV/AIDS, Viral Hepatitis, STD, and TB Prevention.

Additionally, the data related to contraceptive use, abortion rates, and access to comprehensive sexuality education are only part of the picture. The political struggle over reproductive rights is just as essential to understanding this issue. Since the 1973 landmark decision in *Roe v. Wade* legalizing abortion, a well-organized and strategic pro-life movement has systematically worked to limit access to abortion. They have introduced thousands of bills at the state and federal level and have successfully passed almost 1,300 laws. In 2010–2011, with the midterm elections that swept conservative and anti-choice proponents into state legislatures, 1,100 bills were introduced, and 92 passed into law in one year alone.

According to the Guttmacher Institute, these restrictions include laws that:

- Require physicians to perform abortions in hospitals, a procedure typically performed in clinics in 19 states.
- Set gestational limits to prohibit later abortions in 43 states.
- Prohibit "partial-birth" abortions prior to the gestational limits of viability determined by *Roe* in 20 states.
- Restrict the use of public funding through Medicaid for abortion in 33 states.
- Limit private insurance coverage of abortion in 12 states.
- Allow health care providers to refuse to provide abortion services in 45 states.
- Require state-mandated counseling in 18 states that include information about: a purported link between abortion and breast cancer in 5 states, the supposed ability of a fetus to feel pain (in 13 states), or long-term mental health consequences for a woman (in 8 states).
- Require 24–72-hour waiting periods in 27 states, which in 14 states results in two separate trips to get an abortion.
- Require parental involvement (consent or notification) in a minor's decision to have an abortion in 37 states.

With the recent confirmation of Justice Brett Kavanaugh, the anti-abortion movement has successfully set up several direct challenges to *Roe* through the recent 2019 pre-viability abortion restriction bills passed in Alabama, Georgia, Kentucky, Louisiana, Mississippi, Ohio, Missouri, Arkansas, and Utah.

But *Roe* doesn't need to be overturned in order to severely restrict access to abortion services. Some of the state-level abortion restrictions that are currently being legally challenged in court include:

- Prohibiting abortions that are sought for particular reasons (on account of the race, sex, or potential disability of the fetus).
- Mandating the cremation or burial of fetal or embryonic tissue in 3 states.
- Requiring alternative abortion methods that are not the preferred standard of care in 3 states.
- Prohibiting abortion during the pre-viability stage, as early as six weeks after the last period, essentially banning abortion in 9 states.
- Regulations that require doctors to have unnecessary hospital-admitting privileges and clinics to meet hospital-like building

standards, according to a report by the Center for Reproductive Rights.

- Restrictions on discussing abortion in Title X federally funded Family Planning Program.

Ultimately, for as much as this political fight has focused on abortion, a recently released poll conducted by Supermajority and PerryUndem suggests that anti-abortion advocates are significantly more hostile to gender equity and more interested in controlling women than in protecting life.

This increase in anti-abortion legislation has also activated a strong response by reproductive health, rights, and justice advocates. The 2018 midterm elections ushered in more state legislators supportive of reproductive rights. Working with these pro-choice legislators, advocates have introduced and passed proactive legislation to protect and expand access to abortion, contraception, and reproductive health care. This includes state bills to improve insurance coverage by codifying contraceptive benefits in the Affordable Care Act (introduced in 17 states and passed in 6 states), expanding family planning funding, expanding Medicaid coverage to include abortion, and requiring insurance companies that cover pregnancy care also to cover abortion care. At the federal level, the EACH Woman Act (Equal Access in Abortion Coverage in Health Insurance) was introduced in the House and Senate to ensure coverage for abortion for every woman, regardless of income or insurance.

Recommendations and Solutions

In July 2019, more than 80 reproductive health rights and justice organizations endorsed and published a comprehensive Blueprint for Sexual and Reproductive Health, Rights, and Justice. In this policy agenda, they endorse principles to ensure that sexual and reproductive health care is accessible and barrier-free to all people, to increase research and innovation in the field, to promote wellness, and to encourage judges and executive officials to advance sexual and reproductive health rights and justice. Taking an intersectional approach, these organizations are endorsing and promoting an agenda that inextricably links sexual and reproductive health and rights—domestically and globally—to economic justice, voting rights, immigrant rights, LGBTQ liberation, disability justice, and the right to community safety and racial equity.

The aggressive anti-abortion activism and legislative successes of the pro-life movement calls for a federal and state-level policy agenda that is critical to protect, defend, and advance reproductive health care and access in the U.S. At the federal level, this includes:

- Repealing the ban on abortion funding for low-income women (the Hyde Amendment) by passing the EACH Woman Act.
- Repeal restrictions and maintain robust funding of Title X Family Planning funding.
- Allow oral contraceptives to be available over the counter without a prescription.
- Oppose religious refusals that legalize discrimination against abortion care and LGBTQ people.

At the state level, a defensive and proactive policy agenda should include:

- Public and private insurance coverage of all reproductive and sexual health care services.
- Repealing any laws that criminalize people seeking abortions, doctors who perform abortions, any negative pregnancy outcomes like stillbirths and miscarriage, and drug use during pregnancy. Several states have passed laws or criminally prosecuted women for drug use or miscarriages.
- Repealing gestational limits on abortion, including later abortions, which are usually sought when there are medical complications.
- Increasing access to medication abortion (non-surgical abortions), long-acting contraceptives, and over-the-counter contraceptives.

However, separate from these principles and legislative recommendations, there is also a need to refresh and reframe the social movement that engages, activates, and mobilizes people around these issues. A more expansive social movement is needed to counter the pro-life movement's success in reducing access to reproductive and sexual health services, and in culturally and politically limiting women's human rights and autonomy to a religious question about when life begins.

By focusing primarily on abortion, contraception, and sex education, the reproductive rights movement has done a disservice to itself and limited its appeal and effectiveness. Currently, the reproductive rights movement does an imperfect job of offering a comprehensive agenda for the range of issues related to the love, sex, family, and community issues that people care about. Public support for legal abortion has remained high and consistent over the last two decades, with 61 percent of Americans saying abortion should be legal in all or most cases, and only 38 percent saying it should be illegal in all or most cases. Only 12 percent of the population believes it should be illegal in all cases, as demonstrated in a Pew Research Center poll. However, this public support has not translated into an active movement protecting access in the face of a strategic and well-organized opposition that has managed to pass almost 300 laws restricting access in the last five years.

Even as 1 in 4 women will have an abortion during their lives, this movement is not actively appealing to the 3 in 4 women who won't have an abortion, or who are struggling to raise the children they do have, or who are struggling with economic insecurity, violence, food, and housing.

The current movement is framed and perceived as a "woman's movement," excluding men and trans people. As women are encouraged to "come out" and share their abortion stories as a way to de-stigmatize abortion, there is not a similar appeal to men to share the stories of their reproductive lives, the stories of the women in their lives - friends, partners, lovers, sisters, mothers - who've had abortions or whom they've supported through the process. Men are neither calling out and fighting against the patriarchy and sexism that controls and reduces women to their fertility nor are they telling the stories of how their lives were changed by the availability of contraception and abortion care. They are not claiming their role and right to have children and raise those children with dignity. Men, too, have the desire and right to have children and families; and those stories are unvoiced and unshared.

A refresh of this social movement could de-center abortion and contraception, not because they are not important, but because winning them will not be enough to improve people's lives. In *How All Politics Became Reproductive Politics: From Welfare Reform to Foreclosure to Trump,* Laura Briggs argues that all politics from immigration, gay marriage, tax policy, welfare reform, and the subprime housing market are reproductive politics, in that they are about the conditions under which women and families survive, thrive, and reproduce. Without families and communities, there is no economics or politics.

Throughout history, a critical component of systemic oppression has rested on the determination of who counts as a human being and, therefore, who is deserving of rights, respect, and resources. One way enslaved peoples were dehumanized was through rape and the commodification and sale of their bodies and children. In the systemic genocide of Native people, their communities, culture, and families were destroyed by tearing children away from their families and putting them in boarding schools. An immigration system that is only interested in exploiting labor is separating families, women, and children, and detaining them in cages today. LGBTQ people's humanity is denied through stigmatizing and punishing who they love, the kind of sex they enjoy, and the people with whom they want to form families. Poor people are considered less deserving of dignity and support in loving and raising children by virtue of their poverty, while differently abled bodies are desexualized and stigmatized. It is no surprise that the phrase "Black Lives Matter" has been such a resonant call to fight for the worth, value, and humanity of Black people as it is a call for Black people to be included in the category of human.

In an ongoing contestation between people and profits, a reframed movement that fights for all the love, sex, family, and community that people need to survive and thrive could be powerful. It could de-silo movements for climate change, sexual harassment, living wages, housing and gentrification, trans rights, and immigrant rights.

While the current narrative of the reproductive rights movement has narrowed to the medical and health-related concerns of abortion and contraception, the broader fight is over whose love is legally recognized and socially supported; what forms of sex (and with whom) are publicly approved; which types of families are allowed to form, be protected, and resourced; and ultimately how communities form around what identity, values, and systems. Abortion and contraception come nowhere near to capturing the breadth of the battle before us and are even less effective in creatively and inclusively fueling the struggle.

While there are important political and policy battles ahead to protect access to abortion and contraception, the real fight is for the soul of humanity, not just women. Will we value profits more than people, some people more than others? By reframing our fight across a more comprehensive agenda that includes love, sex, family, and community for all, we have the opportunity to appeal to a broader base that can build the political power to ensure access to abortion, protect women's autonomy and self-determination, and ensure that all families and communities survive and thrive.

Key Resources

Beckwith, Francis J. 2007. *Defending Life: A Moral and Legal Case Against Abortion Choice.* New York, NY: Cambridge University Press.

Briggs, Laura. 2017. *How All Politics Became Reproductive Politics: From Welfare Reform to Foreclosure to Trump.* Oakland, CA: University of California Press.

Finer, Lawrence B., and Mia R. Zolna. 2016. "Declines in Unintended Pregnancy in the United States, 2008–2011." *New England Journal of Medicine* 374(9):843–852. https://doi.org/10.1056/NEJMsa1506575.

Flavin, Jeanne. 2009. *Our Bodies, Our Crimes: The Policing of Women's Reproduction in America.* New York, NY: New York University Press.

Grimes, David A., and Linda G. Brandon. 2014. *Every Third Woman in America: How Legal Abortion Transformed Our Nation.* Carolina Beach, NC: Daymark Publishing.

Gurr, Barbara A. 2014. *Reproductive Justice: The Politics of Health Care for Native American Women.* New Brunswick, NJ: Rutgers University Press.

Jones, Rachel K., and Jenna Jerman. 2017. "Population Group Abortion Rates and Lifetime Incidence of Abortion: United States, 2008–2014." *American Journal of Public Health* 107:1904–1909. http://doi.org/10.2105/AJPH.2017.304042.

Kavnaugh, Megan L., and Jenna Jerman. 2018. "Contraceptive Method Use in the United States: Trends and Characteristics between 2008 and 2014." *Contraception* 97(1):14–21. https://doi.org/j.contraception.2017.10.003.

Lindberg, Laura D., Isaac Maddow-Zimet, and Heather Boonstra. 2016. "Changes in Adolescents' Receipt of Sex Education, 2006–2013." *Journal of Adolescent Health* 58(6):621–627. https://doi.org/10.1016/j.jadohealth.2016.02.004.

Mason, Carol. 2002. *Killing for Life: The Apocalyptic Narrative of Pro-Life Politics.* Ithaca, NY: Cornell University Press.

Munson, Ziad W. 2010. *The Making of Pro-Life Activists.* Chicago, IL: University of Chicago Press.

Page, Cristina. 2006. *How the Pro-Choice Movement Saved America: Sex, Virtue, and the Way We Live Now.* New York, NY: Basic Books.

Roberts, Dorothy E. 1999. *Killing the Black Body: Race, Reproduction, and the Meaning of Liberty.* New York, NY: Vintage Books.

Ross, Loretta J., and Rickie Solinger. 2017. *Reproductive Justice: A New Vision for the 21st Century.* Oakland, CA: University of California Press.

Silliman, Jael, Marlene Gerber Fried, Loretta J. Ross, and Elena R. Gutiérrez. 2004. *Undivided Rights: Women of Color Organizing for Reproductive Justice.* Chicago, IL: Haymarket Books.

Stevenson, Robin. 2019. *My Body My Choice: The Fight for Abortion Rights.* Victoria, BC: Orca Book Publishers.

FIVE

In Pursuit of Justice in U.S. Health Care Policy: Pathways to Universal Coverage

Jennifer Roebuck Bulanda and Amelia Pittman

The Problem

Nearly a decade since the contentious passage of the 2010 Patient Protection and Affordable Care Act (ACA), which aimed to expand Americans' access to health insurance, the legislation remains highly controversial. Several attempts to repeal and replace the law failed in 2017, but legislative and executive action have altered the law in fundamental ways since then. Public opinion on the ACA has remained divided since its passage, with about 40 percent of the U.S. public reporting an unfavorable view both immediately after its passage in 2010 and in mid-2019. Instead of the ACA ushering in reform and subsequent stability for the health care system, it does not function the way it was originally intended and Americans have not coalesced around it. This has set the stage for a continued battle for health care reform.

Notably, the ACA did not fundamentally reshape the U.S. health care system. Prior to the ACA, the U.S. was the only developed nation without universal health care, and it retains that distinction even post-reform. Americans receive health insurance through a labyrinthic and patchwork-like system, in which one's age, economic situation, and employment status dictate coverage. About half of Americans receive insurance through an employer (whether their own or a partner's/parent's employer), coverage which is generally terminated upon retirement or changing jobs. After turning 65, the vast majority of older Americans are shuttled into a different health insurance system, receiving their coverage through the federal Medicare program. About a quarter of Americans receive coverage through the Medicaid program, a public health insurance program for people with low income that is funded jointly by the state and federal government. Although the

ACA attempted to extend Medicaid coverage to all Americans with income up to 138 percent of the federal poverty line, 14 states have not expanded their Medicaid coverage as of July 2019. Therefore, inconsistencies in eligibility for Medicaid persist across states, with some states imposing work requirements on recipients, limiting eligibility to certain groups, and/or drawing eligibility thresholds even lower than the federal poverty line. The ACA also introduced a new way for Americans without insurance from an employer or governmental program to obtain health insurance: they can now purchase it from a private insurance company through the Marketplace, a government website allowing individuals to compare plans and enroll in a policy directly, with tax subsidies available on a sliding scale to help uninsured Americans afford their premiums. The ACA mandated that all uninsured individuals (with some exemptions) purchase insurance and stipulated that insurers are no longer allowed to deny coverage based on pre-existing conditions. Although the ACA yielded reform, it did not achieve universal coverage and enduring injustices in access to health care remain. The next election cycle will be crucial in determining what direction the U.S. health care system moves.

The Research Evidence

Census Bureau estimates show a consistent decline in the number of uninsured since full implementation of the ACA, from over 49 million Americans in 2010 to approximately 28 million in 2017. Although efforts in Congress throughout 2017 to repeal and replace the ACA were unsuccessful, the 2017 tax reform legislation effectively removed the individual mandate that required uninsured individuals to acquire insurance. This, coupled with executive action that substantially cut funding for outreach and enrollment assistance and allowed states to add requirements for Medicaid coverage (e.g., employment requirements) or seek waivers that circumvented some of the protective features of the ACA, resulted in an increase in the number of uninsured for the first time since 2013. The Congressional Budget Office estimates that this reversal will continue, with a total of 35 million Americans being uninsured by 2029.

As of 2019, approximately 10 percent of Americans lack insurance. Although those without insurance are a heterogeneous group, uninsured for diverse and complex reasons, inequities in access by social factors such as socioeconomic status, race-ethnicity, age, and citizenship status are clear. Current estimates from the Kaiser Family Foundation (KFF) suggest that about 15 million (55 percent) of the uninsured are eligible for insurance through a public program such as Medicaid, or to receive tax credits to help them purchase insurance through the Marketplace. Another 2.5 million are in the coverage gap because their state did not expand its Medicaid program. Almost 2 million uninsured Americans have income above the threshold for ACA tax credits, and thus there is no provision to help them purchase insurance from the Marketplace, and 3.8 million are ineligible to use the Exchange to purchase insurance because their employer offers them insurance (though the cost of this insurance may not be financially feasible for them). Another 4 million are ineligible due to their immigration status. Immigrants without documentation are not eligible for public insurance programs such as Medicaid, nor are they eligible to purchase insurance through the Marketplace. Even immigrants who are legal U.S. residents face restrictions, such as the requirement that one must wait five years after receiving lawful status before being Medicaid eligible.

In addition to socioeconomic and citizenship status inequities in insurance access, there are also disparities in access by race-ethnicity and age. These disparities narrowed after ACA implementation, but did not disappear. In 2017, 7 percent of non-Hispanic White individuals under age 65 were uninsured, compared to 11 percent of Black individuals, 19 percent of Hispanic individuals, and 22 percent of American Indian and Alaskan Native individuals. The states that expanded Medicaid showed the greatest progress in narrowing these gaps. However, data show that gains in coverage for some race-ethnic groups have stalled or reversed following recent changes to the legislation. Similarly, Georgetown University's Center for Children and Families found a steady decrease in the number of uninsured children from 2008 until 2016, but the trend reversed for the first time in 2017.

Recommendations and Solutions

Addressing the pervasive inequities discussed in this chapter is imperative in order to move toward a more just system. Repealing the ACA, which has served as a political buzzword throughout multiple election cycles, not only fails to remedy disparities in access, but exacerbates them. Rolling back protections for pre-existing conditions and imposing restrictions on Medicaid access result in increasing the number of uninsured individuals as well as increasing disparities in who has access. For example, KFF estimates that 27 percent of U.S. adults under age 65 have a pre-existing condition that would have resulted in denial of coverage in the individual market prior to the ACA, and lower-income and race-ethnic minority individuals are more likely to have pre-existing conditions.

The systems of other high-income nations, all of which have achieved universal access, can be instructive for understanding potential alternatives. These systems are generally structured in one of three ways: as single-payer systems (in which all citizens are provided with a single government-run health insurance plan), multi-payer systems that include private insurance companies (but in which the private insurance companies are subject to strict government regulations, such as price controls and an inability to profit on basic care), or fully socialized medicine (in which the government owns the health care facilities and employs the health care providers). As a system of fully socialized medicine is unlikely to be politically feasible in the U.S. at the current time, we focus on the first two systems as potential pathways to universal coverage in the U.S. in the near future.

Universal Coverage through a Multi-Payer System

The U.S. already has a multi-payer insurance system, though coverage is not universal; numerous private insurance companies as well as several public insurance programs (e.g., Medicare, Medicaid, TRICARE) provide health insurance coverage to about 90 percent of Americans. Advocates for retaining a multi-payer system generally support the idea that competition between insurance providers should promote lower cost and increased innovation and favor the role of private business in providing insurance benefits rather than a government-run program. Some recent legislative efforts have focused on moving toward universal coverage while retaining a multi-payer system by shoring up the Affordable Care Act, such as increasing the subsidies available to help people purchase coverage on the Marketplace and ensuring Medicaid expansion in more states.

Those unsupportive of a multi-payer system generally argue that these systems drive up complexity and administrative costs, which Gaffney and colleagues assert "robs patients and providers of time, money, and morale" (2016: 987). Others argue that the pursuit of profit in health care is unjust and inappropriate. Retaining a multi-payer system also constrains patients' choice of and relationship with their health care providers. Enrollees are only able to choose providers in their insurance plan's network, which often shifts when their employer changes insurance companies/plans, when insurance companies renegotiate contracts with providers, or when employees lose or change jobs. Enrollees may incur substantial and sometimes unexpected costs when using out-of-network providers or when receiving care from multiple providers, such as during surgery or emergency care, in which one provider is in their network but another is not. Detractors of the multi-payer system also point out that incremental expansion of the ACA will still not reach everyone; Drew Altman of KFF points out that over 50 percent of the uninsured population today are eligible for ACA assistance or for Medicaid, but are still not enrolled.

Finally, some argue that continuing the U.S. multi-payer system does not adequately address the problem of affordability. Although progress has been made on uninsurance, a sizable number of Americans continue to grapple with being *under*insured. The average share of premiums paid by employees for employer-sponsored health insurance coverage continues to rise, and employers increasingly utilize high-deductible insurance policies as a mechanism to cut costs. The Kaiser Family Foundation reports that, between 2008 and 2018, the total premium paid by employees for family coverage increased by 55 percent, an increase that has outpaced inflation and increases in wages. In 2018, the average family with employer health insurance coverage spent about $4,700 in premiums and $3,000 in cost sharing (deductibles, co-insurance/co-payments), for a total of nearly $8,000 in total out-of-pocket health costs. And disparities in coverage are clear: Lower-income workers tend to have poorer coverage from their employers with greater cost sharing, which makes out-of-pocket expenses even higher for those with lower socioeconomic status, who are also more likely to be race-ethnic minorities.

A number of other high-income nations utilize a multi-payer system to achieve universal coverage, including Germany, Switzerland, and Japan. However, in those countries, there is substantially more government regulation of insurance companies and the overall system than is the case in the U.S. In some countries, all insurance companies are non-profit and the government sets reimbursement prices for services. There are also government mandates that all citizens enroll in an insurance plan, a feature of the ACA which garnered lower support than other provisions and which is no longer enforced following 2017 legislation. Although some see the retention of private insurance companies through a multi-payer system as the pathway to universal coverage that is most likely to receive sufficient public and political support in the U.S., it remains unclear whether Americans will find palatable the government regulation of insurance companies that would be necessary to expand the system universally and equitably to all U.S. residents. If not, the system would retain some of the same glaring injustices that currently characterize it.

Universal Coverage through a Single-Payer System

A single-payer system offers an alternate pathway to universal coverage. Such a system would fundamentally overhaul the structure of the U.S. system, establishing one singular insurance program covering all Americans. Rather than creating a completely new public insurance program, this would likely happen through the expansion of the existing Medicare program, which currently provides near-universal coverage to Americans age 65 and over. Advocates of single-payer programs point to the equitable treatment of all U.S. residents in such a system. Coverage is not dependent on social factors such as age, income, or employment status; instead, all individuals are covered by the same policy with the same provisions. Supporters of a single-payer system also point to cost savings in the form of reduced administrative costs (for example, providers would no longer have to deal with the minutiae of billing numerous different insurance companies) and elimination of profit pursuit by the private insurance companies.

Several other high-income nations have successfully achieved universal coverage with such a system. Canada and Taiwan both have a national health insurance model in which all citizens are enrolled. Citizens in these countries express a higher degree of satisfaction with their system than do Americans. In fact, Americans currently enrolled in the Medicare system express a higher degree of satisfaction in their health insurance coverage than Americans enrolled in private, employer-provided insurance. Among Medicare recipients, 95 percent rate their coverage as "good" or "excellent." Only 5 percent rate their coverage as "not so good" or "poor" versus 15 percent of Americans with employer-provided private health insurance.

Detractors of a single-payer system generally dislike the expanded role of government, see the loss of private insurance as a loss of individual choice for consumers and a loss of efficiency through competition, fear that the expansion of Medicare will only exacerbate its projected solvency issues, and/or are concerned by the increase in taxes that would be necessary to support such a system. Such a shift would also have important implications for health care providers and health care settings, which depend on the generally higher reimbursement rates of private insurance to offset lower average reimbursement from Medicare. Current estimates show that numerous small hospitals would be insolvent under the current Medicare reimbursement rates and some physicians, particularly specialists, would see declines in pay. Broader adjustments to the system, such as through revisions to

Medicare's reimbursement rates or subsidized medical education, would be necessary to address these projections.

The structure and function of a single-payer model in the U.S. would vary widely depending on its design, including its funding mechanism, the degree of cost sharing on the part of recipients, and the role of private insurance in the new system. Current legislators' proposals for a single-payer system differ substantially with regard to services covered, ranging from a baseline set of basic services to a fairly comprehensive array of health care that includes vision, dental, and long-term care insurance, and the level of cost sharing, varying from some co-payments, premiums, and/or deductibles to none at all. Tax increases would be necessary to fund a national insurance system, but the cost of increased income taxes would be offset by reductions in premiums and/or deductibles and co-pays/co-insurance. Whether this would result in overall additional costs or cost savings to the average consumer depends on the policy proposed. It is, however, vital that the funding scheme for a single-payer program ensures that the program is affordable to those with lower socioeconomic status in order to make the system equitable. In addition, different proposals have different implications for private insurance; some would offer completely comprehensive coverage with no role for private insurance whereas others would offer universal baseline coverage with the option to receive from employers or individually purchase more expansive coverage. Specific implications for justice in access and coverage would depend on the specific policy design, but taxes to fund the program and cost sharing should be progressive, such that the program remains affordable for lower-income Americans. In addition, comprehensive rather than baseline coverage should be offered in order to eliminate stratification in coverage.

The Need for Greater Public Education on Health Insurance

It is imperative that Americans engage in informed debate on health care reform. Unfortunately, research conducted by KFF shows low levels of health insurance literacy among the general public: many Americans do not understand key aspects of the current insurance system, much less potential alternate systems. Americans are ill-equipped to assess the veracity of politicians' statements about the benefits and limitations of different reform efforts, and this lack of knowledge has often been exploited for political ends, further driving injustice in the system.

In 2019, polls showed that about half of Americans favor a national health insurance system in which all Americans would get their insurance through a single government plan. However, the amount of support changes, sometimes dramatically, when respondents are informed of different facets of such a system. For example, when informed that they would not be able to keep their private insurance policy under such a system, support drops significantly. A greater share of Americans support incrementally building on the ACA than moving to a single-payer system, but support again shifts when respondents are informed of specific features. In addition, terminology used imprecisely by politicians sometimes obfuscates rather than clarifies. "Medicare for All," for example, is a buzzword sometimes used to refer to a single-payer plan in which all Americans would have Medicare as their insurance policy, and at other times used to describe plans in which Medicare could be offered as an option to certain groups (e.g., those near retirement, those eligible to purchase insurance through the Marketplace, or anyone not otherwise eligible for another public insurance program such as Medicaid). In this scenario, "Medicare for All" does not mean transitioning to a single-payer system, but rather to the retention of a multi-payer system in which Medicare exists as an option alongside other private and/or public insurers. These discrepancies in meaning and understanding, and Americans' general inability to make sense of them, make widespread public education on health insurance a prerequisite for any productive debate on the subject.

The U.S. health care system stands at a crossroads. Though there is general agreement that change is necessary, consensus on what the change should be remains lacking. The void in public understanding of different health insurance systems and the implications of their different structures represents an important area to which researchers, policy-makers, academicians, and applied social scientists can contribute. In addition to working to increase Americans' health insurance literacy, it is imperative that inequities in the current system remain at the forefront of the debate, and that the principal goal of reform be the pursuit of justice. The 2020 election will likely determine the future direction of the U.S. health care system, and presents an important focal point for advocacy efforts.

Key Resources

Alker, Joan and Olivia Pham. 2018. "Nation's Progress on Children's Health Coverage Reverses Course." Georgetown University Health Policy Institute Center for Children and Families. (https://ccf.georgetown.edu/2018/11/21/nations-progress-on-childrens-health-coverage-reverses-course/)

Artiga, Samantha, Kendal Orgera, and Anthony Damico. 2019. "Changes in Health Coverage by Race and Ethnicity since Implementation of the ACA, 2013–2017." (www.kff.org/disparities-policy/issue-brief/changes-in-health-coverage-by-race-and-ethnicity-since-the-aca-2010-2018)

Artiga, Samantha and Maria Diaz. 2019. "Health Coverage and Care of Undocumented Immigrants." (http://files.kff.org/attachment/Issue-Brief-Health-Coverage-and-Care-of-Undocumented-Immigrants)

The Commonwealth Fund. 2019. "International Health Care System Profiles - Country Profiles." (https://international.commonwealthfund.org/countries/)

Dickman, Samuel L., David U. Himmelstein, and Steffie Woolhandler. 2017. "Inequality and the Health Care System in the U.S.A." *Lancet, 389,* 1431–1441. doi: 10.1016/S0140-6736(17)30398-7

Fehr, Rachel, Anthony Damico, Larry Levitt, Gary Claxton, Cynthia Cox, and Karen Pollitz. 2018. "Mapping Pre-existing Conditions across the U.S." Kaiser Family Foundation. (http://files.kff.org/attachment/Issue-Brief-Mapping-Pre-existing-Conditions-across-the-US)

Gaffney, Adam, Steffie Woolhandler, Marcia Angell, and David U. Himmelstein. 2016. "Moving Forward from the Affordable Care Act to a Single-Payer System." *American Journal of Public Health, 106,* 987–988.

Garfield, Rachel, Kendal Orgera, & Anthony Damico. 2019. "The Uninsured and the ACA: A Primer – Key Facts about Health Insurance and the Uninsured amidst Changes to the Affordable Care Act." (http://files.kff.org/attachment/The-Uninsured-and-the-ACA-A-Primer-Key-Facts-about-Health-Insurance-and-the-Uninsured-amidst-Changes-to-the-Affordable-Care-Act)

Kirzinger, Ashley, Cailey Munana, and Mollyann Brodie. 2019. "KFF Health Tracking Poll - July 2019: The Future of the ACA and Possible Changes to the Current System." Kaiser Family Foundation. (https://www.kff.org/health-reform/poll-finding/kff-health-tracking-poll-july-2019/)

Neuman, Tricia, Karen Pollitz, and Jennifer Tolbert. 2018. "Medicare-for-All and Public Plan Buy-In Proposals: Overview and Key Issues." (http://files.kff.org/attachment/Issue-Brief-Medicare-for-All-and-Public-Buy-In-Proposals-Overview-and-Key-Issues)

Rae, Matthew, Rebecca Copeland, and Cynthia Cox. 2019. "Tracking the rise in premium contributions and cost-sharing for families with large employer coverage." Kaiser Family Foundation. (https://www.healthsystemtracker.org/brief/tracking-the-rise-in-premium-contributions-and-cost-sharing-for-families-with-large-employer-coverage/)

SIX

The Problem of Unpaid Parental Leave

Ronald E. Bulanda and Jennifer Roebuck Bulanda

The Problem

The United States is the only high-income country – and, along with Papua New Guinea, one of only two countries worldwide – with no national paid maternity leave policy. Although six states have legislation mandating statewide paid parental leave and some employees receive paid leave as a fringe benefit from their employer, access to paid parental leave remains unjust. Statistics from the U.S. Department of Labor show that only about 16 percent of workers in the private sector have employer-provided paid family leave, and this figure drops to 7 percent of workers who earn less than $14 an hour. Similarly, parents who struggle the most to meet the financial needs of raising children are the least likely to have access to any workplace accommodations, and research shows this burden is disproportionately borne by women with lower levels of income and education.

The 1993 Family and Medical Leave Act (FMLA) established national unpaid family leave regulations, but it has resulted in notable inequities. The FMLA allows employees up to 12 weeks of unpaid leave to care for a newborn child or to tend to the illness of one's relative or self. However, only employees working for an employer with 50 or more employees and who have worked at least 1,250 hours over the past 12 months are eligible. According to estimates from the Kaiser Family Foundation, these exemptions mean that only about 60 percent of Americans are eligible to use FMLA leave. Even for those who are eligible, the leave is unpaid, often resulting in parents forgoing or abbreviating their leave. A Pew Research Center poll showed that, among those who take parental leave, the majority did not take as much as they needed or wanted; when asked the reason, 69 percent indicated they could not afford to lose more wages or salary. The failure to provide paid leave to new parents is a significant social justice issue with implications for successfully balancing work and family obligations. Moreover, given the gendered division of household labor (including parenting), as well as gender inequalities in the workplace (e.g., the pay gap and glass ceiling), the absence of a mandate to provide paid leave reflects a form of institutional discrimination for working mothers. Given these inequities, there is a clear need to revise our federal work leave policy to promote healthier families and workers, while also establishing more egalitarian work-family arrangements for employed parents.

Though numerous legislative attempts to establish a national paid family leave policy over the past decade have failed to garner sufficient political support, President Trump's stated support for paid family leave has changed the political climate. Both Republican and Democratic legislators have introduced paid parental leave legislation in Congress since 2017. Americans also seem poised to support paid family leave legislation; a 2017 Pew Research Center poll finds that 82 percent of Americans agree that paid leave should be granted to mothers and 69 percent agree it should be given to fathers following the birth or adoption of a child. However, there are substantial differences in the components and function of potential parental leave policies. These differences are vital to consider in order to design a just policy.

The Research Evidence

Given the benefits associated with paid leave, the risks associated with a lack of parental leave, and the fact that virtually every nation around the world has adopted some type of paid parental leave policy, it is particularly striking that the U.S. has failed to do so. This lack of support for families has significant implications for children and parents' physical, mental, and financial well-being. Research by Glass, Simon, and Andersson (2016) shows that family-friendly policies, particularly in the form of paid leave, significantly affect the happiness of parent workers, and that paid leave reduces the long-term employment costs and fosters greater parent-child bonds following the transition to parenthood. Research from scholars at the Institute for Health and Social Policy at McGill University and the Institute on Urban Health Research at Northeastern University found that paid leave in 141 countries is correlated with lower infant mortality rates, net of each nation's economy and expenditures. Reviews of the literature by a pair of distinguished professors in sociology and economics found that paid leave also promoted more well-visits to doctors and higher immunization rates, which translates into improved child health.

Longer periods of leave are associated with reduced postpartum depression and better physical health for mothers, and are predictive of higher rates and durations of breastfeeding.

Paid parental leave also has economic benefits, such as reducing a family's risk of falling into poverty after the birth of a child. Scholars who authored a comprehensive assessment of California's policy argue paid leave was associated with a greater likelihood that mothers returned to work, decreased employee turnover rates, and higher worker morale. However, taking parental leave in the U.S. remains financially risky. Pew Research Center poll data show that, of those who received only some or no pay when taking leave, 41 percent took on debt, 27 percent put off paying bills, 21 percent went on public assistance, and 19 percent borrowed money from family/friends.

One of the barriers to enacting paid parental leave in the U.S. is concern about the consequences for employers. In the absence of federal legislation on paid leave, California, New York, New Jersey, Massachusetts, Washington, Rhode Island, and the District of Columbia have passed statewide legislation on paid leave. Research on these state programs has yielded important preliminary data about the consequences of paid family leave. An analysis by the Center for Economic and Policy Research of California's 2003 Paid Family Leave (PFL) program, the first state-wide paid leave policy in the U.S., shows that concerns that the program would produce onerous costs on employers and particularly small businesses were unfounded. Most employers reported minimal or no impact on their businesses, and over 85 percent of employers reported no effects or positive effects on profitability/performance, productivity, turnover, and employee morale. In fact, small businesses were actually less likely than larger businesses to report negative effects. Over 90 percent of employers responding to the survey said they were not aware of any reports of abuse of the program. In fact, in some instances, there are cost savings for businesses that already had established paid leave policies, in that they no longer had to self-fund these paid leaves and could instead use the state PFL program to fund employee leave.

Recommendations and Solutions

Julie Suk's (2013) review of Justice Ruth Bader Ginsburg's dealings with FMLA and related court cases highlighted the complexities of establishing more equitable arrangements for women at work and at home, and identifies the solution to be a policy for pregnancies and maternity leave that is both adequate and sustainable. Currently, the unpaid leave component of FMLA reflects an inadequate policy. It is sustainable on the basis that the workers, particularly women who already receive lower pay than men, sacrifice their income to care for their families, or shoulder the burdens of work and pregnancy/newborns by not utilizing any/all of their unpaid leave. One feasible solution is to establish a national system to support paid parental leave. Yet, there are important considerations in implementing such a system. Based on the research evidence reviewed in this chapter, a socially just paid maternity leave policy in the U.S. should be attentive to the following:

1. Provide Parents with at Least 24 Weeks of 100 Percent Paid Maternity Leave

Parents need sufficient time to recover from childbirth, bond with and care for new children, and adjust to a major life change. Current bills proposed by legislators in multiple political parties range from 6 to 12 weeks of partially paid parental leave. This length of leave falls far short of median parental leave time in other high-income countries and is also lower than the parental leave offered by a number of low-income countries. In their analysis of 185 countries, Addati, Cassirer, and Gilchrist (2014) find that only 15 percent provide fewer than 12 weeks of paid maternity leave. According to the Pew Research Center, the shortest amount of paid leave offered by any of the other OECD countries is about two months; the majority offer over 20 weeks of paid leave for new parents, and about a quarter of OECD countries offer over a year of paid leave.

Wage replacement rates for proposed U.S. legislation generally range from 50 to 75 percent of pay. This is similar to the wage replacement offered by most of the state programs that have been enacted thus far in the U.S. Research suggests that such reductions in pay create inequities in who is able to utilize the leave. In the states that have mandated a paid leave policy, lower-income workers are less likely to take paid family leave than higher-income workers, as the partial wages make it financially untenable. In an analysis of California's program by the Center for Economic and Policy Research, the majority of workers who indicated they were aware of California's paid leave program but did not apply though eligible felt the wage replacement was too low. As of 2018, several countries, including Austria, Chile, Estonia, Luxembourg, Mexico, Poland, and Spain, offer 12–20 weeks of leave at 100 percent wage replacement. These countries have demonstrated a willingness and ability to implement a system of offering full wage compensation for a maternity leave that is at least as long as the 12-week unpaid leave period currently provided via FMLA. Given that the majority of high-income countries offer at least 20 weeks of fully paid leave, we suggest that efforts to initiate paid leave in the U.S. focus on establishing, at minimum, six months (24 weeks) of fully paid leave.

2. Fund Paid Parental Leave through a System in which Costs are Not Borne Solely by Individuals or Employers

Ideally, parental leave would be funded using the social insurance model utilized by most high-income nations. In this model, payroll taxes from employers and employees contribute to a social insurance fund from which workers then withdraw benefits when they qualify for parental leave. This functions similarly to employee/employer contributions to the disability system in the U.S. Though legislation establishing such a system has been proposed in Congress, the idea of raising payroll taxes and creating a new government-run program is unlikely to receive sufficient support in either the executive or legislative branches of government. Americans appear to have a difficult time coalescing around a single financing strategy, though the broadest public support exists for optional programs such as tax credits to employers that establish paid leave or allowing workers to set aside pre-tax contributions. However, research suggests a majority of Americans may support establishing a social insurance program. In a 2016 Pew Research Center poll, 62 percent of Americans somewhat or strongly favored providing paid leave through payroll contributions from employees and employers.

The key feature differentiating the legislation to establish a paid parental leave policy in the U.S. has been who will fund the leave. Options for funding paid parental leave outside of the social insurance model include employer mandates (for example, in which the employer is required to provide paid leave and also to assume the costs), incentivizing employer programs by providing tax credits to those that choose to provide paid leave, funding by the government from general revenue, joint funding from both employee and employer payroll taxes, and funding solely from employees.

One example of self-funded leave is allowing employees to establish a savings account with pre-tax contributions from which they can later withdraw during leave. Programs allowing workers to accumulate pre-tax savings for parental leave are limited in that individuals in their childbearing years are often at a life stage that also includes home downpayment and mortgages, payments on student loan debt, and lower-wage and more tenuous work as they take on entry-level jobs during the transition from education to full-time work. In addition, a substantial number of births are unplanned, thus not allowing parents the time to accumulate sufficient funds.

Another example of self-funded leave allows workers to access their Social Security funds early to fund their parental leave. Two recent proposals in Congress utilize this funding strategy; in exchange for early access of up to three months of Social Security funds, recipients would receive reduced or delayed Social Security payments in later life. Advocates for using the Social Security system to fund paid leave point to the fact that it does not require raising current taxes or adding new taxes, does not require any funding from employers, and places personal responsibility for parental leave on the parents themselves. Opponents point to the fact that allowing individuals to withdraw funds from Social Security may worsen Social Security's solvency and sets a new precedent that individuals should use Social Security to fund non-retirement-related expenses. This type of funding mechanism could also exacerbate current disparities in later-life financial well-being, such as the lower lifetime earnings and Social Security benefits of women with children compared to those without children, as documented in research by scholars at the Center for Retirement Research at Boston College. Older women are already more likely to be in poverty than older men, in large part due to the time they have taken away from the labor force for caregiving responsibilities, which not only lowers wages but also the contributions that they and/or their employer make towards their pensions and Social Security. Requiring individuals to self-fund their paid leave by withdrawing their Social Security funds early penalizes parents through their retirement benefits, particularly those with larger families, and will likely exacerbate inequities in financial well-being during the later life course.

3. Include Equal Coverage for Mothers/Fathers/Partners and Extend Coverage to Those Doing Full-Time, Part-Time, Temporary, or Self-Employed Labor

Equitable paid parental leave policy means coverage for all workers. All parents should receive time off to care for their children, regardless of sex, type of employment, or hours worked. An Urban Institute review finds that fathers who take parental leave are more involved in childcare even after the leave has ended and their leave is also associated with lower depressive symptoms among their partners. Hence, extending coverage for both partners may ultimately help children experience more intimate bonds with a second parental figure over a longer period of time, while also contributing to a healthier work–family balance. Bonds and involvement with two parental figures promote more positive outcomes (e.g., self-esteem) in children, and less work–family conflict has positive implications for workplace morale and discord within the home. Given the added benefits of extending coverage to mothers and fathers in heterosexual unions, combined with the intent of promoting a more fair and just policy than currently exists in the U.S., paid leave should also apply to parents in same-sex couples with new/young children. In a time when same-sex marriages are now legal across all states, the need for such policy coverage is sure to grow in demand.

4. Frame Paid Parental Leave as a Social Justice Issue Affecting All of U.S. Society, Not Just Parents

As the Urban Institute points out, establishing a self-funded paid parental leave system reifies the belief that the costs of children should be borne singularly by parents rather than by the broader society. As fertility rates drop below replacement rate in high-income countries, there has been substantial attention to the ways in which children contribute valuable resources to society: they are the next generation of societal leaders, educators, and workers, and a country's economic productivity and financial solvency are dependent on continued childbearing and investments in childrearing. Many of the countries with expansive paid parental leave policies have increased the generosity of their programs in order to encourage families to have more children in the wake of below-replacement-level fertility rates. Recent trends in the U.S. fertility rate suggest the country may be following a similar trend. Establishing a social insurance program, consistent with the model used by most other high-income nations with paid parental leave policies, would share the cost of paid leave between all employees and employers, promoting a stable birth rate and parental investments in children that benefit our economy and society in a multitude of ways.

Key Resources
Addati, Laura, Naomi Cassirer, and Katherine Gilchrist. 2014. "Maternity and Paternity at Work: Law and Practice across the World." Geneva: International Labor Office.

Brainerd, Jackson. 2017. "Paid Family Leave in the States." National Conference of State Legislatures. http://www.ncsl.org/research/labor-and-employment/paid-family-leave-in-the-states.aspx

Dagher, Rada K., Patricia M. McGovern, and Bryan E. Dowd. 2014. "Maternity Leave Duration and Postpartum Mental and Physical Health: Implications for Leave Policies." *Journal of Health Politics, Policy, & Law* 39(2):369–416.

Gault, Barbara, Heidi Hartmann, Ariane Hegewisch, Jessica Milli, and Lindsey Reichlin. 2014. "Paid Parental Leave in the United States." Institute for Women's Policy Research. https://digitalcommons.ilr.cornell.edu/cgi/viewcontent.cgi?article=2608&context=key_workplace

Glass, Jennifer, Robin W. Simon, and Matthew A. Andersson. 2016. "Parenthood and Happiness: Effects of Work-Family Reconciliation Policies in 22 OECD Countries." *American Journal of Sociology* 122(3):886–929.

Horowitz, Juliana M., Kim Parker, Nikki Graf, and Gretchen Livingston. 2017. "Americans Widely Support Paid Family and Medical Leave, but Differ Over Specific Policies." Pew Research Center. https://www.pewsocialtrends.org/2017/03/23/americans-widely-support-paid-family-and-medical-leave-but-differ-over-specific-policies

Isaacs, Julia, Olivia Healy, and H. Elizabeth Peters. 2017. "Paid Family Leave in the United States: Time for a New National Policy." Washington, D.C.: Urban Institute. https://www.urban.org/sites/default/files/publication/90201/paid_family_leave_0.pdf

Kelly, Erin L. and Alexandra Kalev. 2006. "Managing Flexible Work Arrangements in U.S. Organizations: Formalized Discretion or 'A Right to Ask.'" *Socio-Economic Review* 4(3):379–416.

Kurani, Nisha, Usha Ranji, Alina Salganicoff, and Matthew Rae. 2017. "Paid Family Leave and Sick Days in the U.S.: Findings from the 2016 Kaiser/HRET Employer Health Benefits Survey." Kaiser Family Foundation. https://www.kff.org/report-section/paid-family-leave-and-sick-days-in-the-u-s-findings-from-the-2016-kaiserhret-employer-health-benefits-survey-data-note/

Livingston, Gretchen. 2016. "Among 41 Nations, U.S. is the Outlier When It Comes to Paid Parental Leave." Pew Research Center. https://www.pewresearch.org/fact-tank/2016/09/26/u-s-lacks-mandated-paid-parental-leave/.

"Looking after baby; Paid family leave." 2019. *The Economist* *432*(9152):22. https://www.economist.com/united-states/2019/ 07/18/america-is-the-only-rich-country-without-a-law-on-paid- leave-for-new-parents

Milkman, Ruth and Eileen Appelbaum. 2013. *Unfinished Business: Paid Family Leave in California and the Future of U.S. Work-Family Policy*, Ithaca, NY: Cornell University Press.

National Partnership for Women & Families. February 2019. "The Family and Medical Insurance Leave (FAMILY) Act." https://www. nationalpartnership.org/our-work/resources/economic-justice/paid- leave/family-act-fact-sheet.pdf

OECD Family Database. 2019. "PF2.1. Parental Leave Systems." https://www.oecd.org/els/soc/PF2_1_Parental_leave_systems.pdf

Suk, Julie C. 2013. "A More Egalitarian Relationship at Home and at Work: Justice Ginsburg's Dissent in Coleman v. Court of Appeals of Maryland." *Harvard Law Review* 127(1):473–477.

SECTION III

Education

Power, Privilege, and #MeToo in Academia: Problems, Policies, and Prevention around Sexual Misconduct

Sarah Jane Brubaker and Brittany Keegan

The Problem

Sexual misconduct is pervasive in society today, and is oftentimes supported by structures and institutions that promote power and privilege for some while increasing the marginalization, and subsequent likelihood of victimization, of others. In 2006, the #MeToo movement was founded to encourage survivors of sexual abuse, particularly women of color, to share their experiences. This movement entered into the public eye after the #MeToo hashtag went viral in October 2017, and continues to show the pervasiveness of sexual misconduct in all areas of social and professional life. It also aims to hold accountable those who commit this type of misconduct.

Academia is no exception to this problem, with sexual misconduct occurring regularly on university campuses as well as within academic professional organizations. Individuals with less power in the academic hierarchy (e.g. students, non-tenured professors, and members of marginalized communities) are more likely to experience sexual misconduct, though, as is the case with sexual misconduct in general, no one is immune.

At the micro level, sexual misconduct harms survivors in multiple ways (e.g. chronic mental, physical, and sexual health problems, substance abuse, relationship problems, and damaged reputations). It can also deny them professional opportunities and even end professional careers. At the macro level, sexual misconduct harms universities and academic professional organizations as a whole. When sexual misconduct takes place, it creates an environment that feels less safe and can bring into question the integrity of the university/organization and its members.

The way in which academia promotes professional hierarchies on the basis of achievement codified through status, rank, and narrow definitions of achievement, and incorporates and recreates social hierarchies based on identity such as gender, sexual identity, race, ethnicity, ability, and others can support an environment in which sexual misconduct takes place. All of these bases for inequality provide the foundation for power dynamics that are reinforced through interactions, policies, and other organizational and structural elements, as well as through cultural assumptions, beliefs, and stereotypes.

While policies may be put into place to help protect individuals against sexual misconduct and to hold universities and academic processional organizations accountable for the behavior of their members, not all of these policies are effective. They may be too brief or vague to be enforceable, or they may lack important components such as reporting procedures, disciplinary actions, or the provision of support for those filing a report (e.g. advocacy or counseling services). In other cases, policies against sexual misconduct may not even exist in particular settings. Furthermore, policies often focus on response and do little to prevent sexual assault from occurring, which many recognize as an area demanding increased focus and attention. Where policies can help facilitate individual reporting and formalize organizational response to sexual assault, truly preventing sexual misconduct from occurring requires comprehensive cultural change.

Therefore, the problem here is two-fold. Not only is sexual misconduct pervasive in academic settings and supported by the culture of academia, but responses are also insufficient. As movements such as #MeToo continue to raise awareness of and demand solutions to this issue, universities and academic professional organizations must take meaningful action.

The Research Evidence

Research indicates that sexual misconduct is prominent in academia; in fact, a 2018 report from the National Academies of Science, Engineering, and Medicine (NASEM) discussed how the academic workplace experiences the second highest rate of sexual harassment, second only to the military. Though related research and public discourse tend to focus on STEM fields, those working in all academic fields can be impacted by sexual misconduct.

On campus, students are particularly at risk. A 2015 study from the Association of American Universities (AAU) found that 11.7 percent of undergraduate and graduate students experienced some form of sexual misconduct on campus, though overall reporting rates ranged from 5 percent to 28 percent depending on the exact type of sexual misconduct in question. In addition, data collected from 1995–2013 by the Bureau of Justice Statistics show that students are less likely to report sexual misconduct to police than members of the general population of similar age. In the AAU study, reasons for students not filing a report included feelings of shame and embarrassment, concerns of experiencing emotional distress during the reporting process, and concerns that nothing would be done in response to the report.

Research has noted the role of power and privilege in experiencing and reporting sexual and other types of misconduct and has found that those with less power and privilege may be more likely to experience such misconduct and more hesitant to file a report, in general as well as in academia. Reports from the National Sexual Violence Resource Center (NSVRC) and the Rape, Abuse & Incest National Network (RAINN) show that survivors from marginalized communities (e.g. people of color, immigrants, and members of the LGBTQ community) and those with fewer economic resources are more at risk of experiencing sexual misconduct. Studies have indicated that they also face more barriers to reporting because of negative cultural stereotypes about their communities, histories of mistreatment by formal institutions leading to mistrust, and lack of information regarding reporting processes (see, for example, a 2011 article from Porter and Williams on "Intimate Violence Among Underrepresented Groups on a College Campus"). To address this issue, policymakers (e.g. the U.S. Department of Justice and the U.S. Department of Education) recommend that special attention be given to support members of marginalized communities in both response and prevention efforts.

Sexual misconduct is also pervasive at academic professional conferences. A 2017 survey of American Political Science Association conference participants conducted by Sapiro and Campbell (2018), for example, found that 30 percent of women and 10 percent of men reported experiencing some form of sexual misconduct (e.g. inappropriate language or looks, experiencing sexual remarks, etc.) while at the conference. One potential reason for this is that many of the risk factors of experiencing sexual misconduct noted by organizations such as the U.S. Department of Justice and the World

Health Organization (alcohol consumption, being in an unfamiliar environment, unbalanced power dynamics, etc.) are present within the typical conference environment.

Many have noted the importance of having policies related to preventing and addressing sexual misconduct in academic settings. A 2014 report from the Centers for Disease Control and Prevention (CDC), for example, discusses the importance of sexual misconduct prevention as well as promising practices for achieving prevention. However, there is also concern that these policies are insufficient and reactionary, focusing more on response rather than on the ultimate goal of prevention. Some studies, such as a 2019 analysis of campus sexual assault policy implementation by Moylan and Hammock, have questioned if the sexual misconduct policies of academic institutions are aligned with their actual practices, i.e., if reform is something that is discussed with little action actually taken.

In the following section, we offer recommendations and solutions for addressing these issues.

Recommendations and Solutions

Here we share some promising practices identified by policymakers, researchers, and practitioners for creating policies against sexual misconduct, as well as suggestions for prevention efforts, to create a safe and inclusive academic environment free from sexual misconduct. Drawing on sociological frameworks, we argue for the need to address *structural*, *cultural*, and *interactional* levels of social life and relevant to academia, in terms of both a) factors that contribute to sexual harassment and b) opportunities for intervention and change.

1. Conduct Surveys of Sexual Misconduct to Collect Data Regarding Prevalence

Universities and academic professional organizations should assess the extent to which their members (faculty, staff, and students) are experiencing these behaviors in their professional activities. Most campuses are now required to conduct annual climate surveys for this purpose, but they typically only collect data from and focus on students, excluding faculty and staff. Furthermore, most professional organizations have not assessed these problems within their own organizations. These data would provide information regarding prevalence and details about the routine activities that place people at risk, i.e., when and where sexual misconduct is happening and the most likely victims and perpetrators. Like the #MeToo movement, this type of assessment can help provide an outlet for those who have experienced sexual misconduct to share their experiences.

2. Use Data to Create and Strengthen Policies for Addressing and Preventing Sexual Misconduct

Once survey data has been collected, universities and academic professional organizations can use this information to guide response and prevention efforts. Findings could be utilized by each individual organization, and the use of standard and validated measures of various types of assault and harassment would allow for comparisons across organizations to compare contexts and identify risk and protective factors. Information regarding both victimization and perpetration is critical to prevention and response. A university or academic professional organization's policies for addressing and preventing sexual misconduct should clearly define sexual misconduct; as an example, the U.S. Equal Employment Opportunity Commission defines sexual harassment as "unwelcome sexual advances, requests for sexual favors, and other verbal comment or physical conduct of a sexual nature." Policies should also articulate expected and unacceptable behaviors, conveying shared cultural expectations and norms. They should also provide survivors with options during the reporting process and acknowledge individual and group differences in power, as well as systematic institutionalized racism, sexism, homophobia, cissexism, ableism, and other forms of oppression. Policies should include detailed information regarding implementation of the policy through specific reporting, investigation, and sanctioning practices as described in the next section.

3. Improve Practices for How Sexual Misconduct is Addressed and Prevented in Academic Settings

This recommendation is broad in scope and applies to both practices involved in implementing policies against sexual misconduct and general practices in which professional and academic organizations engage. While the previous recommendation focuses more on policy, this recommendation focuses more on action.

a. Practices for implementing policies against sexual misconduct should include clear mechanisms and processes for reporting, require investigations to be carried out by impartial individuals with relevant expertise, and articulate methods of sanctioning and holding individuals and organizations accountable. Practices should be clearly articulated that provide various types of support for survivors, based on survivor-centered and trauma-informed approaches. Practices that consider survivors of all identities and experiences, especially those from socially marginalized groups, can empower and address the unique needs of survivors and can lead to higher rates of reporting. These practices include, but are not limited to, offering a number of reporting options, such as informal consultations without launching a formal investigation and confidential reporting options (protecting individuals with less power); including an affirmative consent statement (giving more voice to those with less power); allowing the person making the report to have options throughout the reporting process (empowering survivors); and providing access to support systems such as counselors or advocates (prioritizing the immediate safety and health needs of survivors). These practices may also help to reduce reporting barriers, as they can demonstrate an understanding of the cultural, social, and personal needs and experiences of survivors.

b. Organizations should seek to change professional practices contributing to sexual misconduct. This could be achieved by developing strategies for minimizing the risks for sexual misconduct at conferences through approaches such as bystander-intervention training and awareness, and limiting the dominant presence of alcohol. As professional organizations are in a unique position to create change by educating/training members, according to the 2018 NASEM report, these strategies could first be developed by the academic professional organizations. By demonstrating an awareness of the problem and a motivation to intervene, and reducing the routine and excessive presence of alcohol, organizations may help to prevent harassment from occurring. In their report on preventing sexual misconduct, the CDC recommends that organizations incorporate the following principles of prevention in their efforts, and ensure that their policies and actions:

- are comprehensive,
- provide sufficient dosage (i.e., multiple sessions tend to be better than single sessions),
- are administered by well-trained staff,
- are socioculturally relevant,
- are based in a sound theory of change,
- build on or support positive relationships (i.e., between the participants and their peers, families or communities),
- use varied teaching methods, and
- evaluate outcomes.

4. Address Retaliation by the Perpetrator, University, and/or Organization

Policies should explicitly prohibit retaliation against 1) those who file a report, 2) those who support those filing a report, and 3) those who express concerns about an employee or member when a report has been made public and action is not taken. Despite efforts focused on bystander intervention, we recognize that it can be difficult and risky to speak out against someone with tenure or other forms of privilege and there is a real or perceived risk of losing one's job, position, or status for doing so.

5. Collaborate with Service Providers, Other Organizations/Institutions, and Survivors in Developing Methods to Address and Prevent Sexual Misconduct

Practitioners and researchers (e.g. the CDC) discuss the benefits of collaboration when working to address sexual misconduct. These collaborations may take place across service providers, between service providers and those impacted by sexual assault and sexual harassment, and between institutions such as colleges and universities and community organizations. Collaborations can help to ensure organizations are addressing all relevant concerns of all parties, responding to various needs through specialized areas of expertise, and working together as a community to collectively define and uphold values.

6. Prevent Sexual Misconduct through Culture Change

Universities and academic professional organizations should also consider changing the broader culture of academia to minimize power dynamics. They should seek ways to challenge hierarchical organizational structures reinforcing power differentials that can make individuals with less power dependent on those with more power and vulnerable to their abusive behaviors. Such change could entail rethinking value systems in academia through, for example, placing a greater emphasis on working with students, collaborating with peers, and conducting community-engaged, participatory action and qualitative research rather than traditional forms of quantitative and peer-reviewed research. Reconsidering the competitive and often cutthroat culture of "publish or perish" and pressure to publish only narrowly defined significant findings could prompt overall challenges to unsupportive and unethical environments. They should also question and challenge the taken-for-granted assumptions and behaviors embedded in academia and organizations' reinforcement of social and cultural stereotypes, thereby disrupting normative structures that lead to sexual misconduct. While cultural norms can be difficult to change, individuals and organizations can both play a role. For example, the 2018 NASEM report discussed how professional organizations can be drivers of culture change in their field. In addition, the voices of the #MeToo movement have drawn attention to this issue and have ensured that sexual misconduct in academia and in society as a whole can no longer be ignored.

There is no doubt that sexual misconduct is rampant in academia, and we need to do more to acknowledge, understand, and begin to alleviate the problem through a multi-pronged approach aimed at individual, interpersonal, cultural, and structural action and change. We need to examine the ways academia recreates oppression and marginalization, and to actively and honestly engage in efforts to hold one another accountable, support and protect survivors, and create real and sustainable cultural change. We must listen to the voices of those who have said #MeToo, and work to ensure that their stories drive our policies and actions in combating sexual misconduct.

Key Resources

Armstrong, Elizabeth, Gleckman-Krut, Miriam, and Johnson, Lanora. 2018. "Silence, Power, and Inequality: An Intersectional Approach to Sexual Violence." *Annual Review of Sociology* 44:99–122.

Brubaker, Sarah Jane, Keegan, Brittany, Guadalupe-Diaz, Xavier L., and Beasley, Bre'auna. 2017. "Measuring and Reporting Campus Sexual Assault: Privilege and Exclusion in What We Know and What We Do." *Sociology Compass* 11.

Bursik, Krisanne and Gefter, Julia. 2011. "Still Stable After All These Years: Perceptions of Sexual Harassment in Academic Contexts." *The Journal of Social Psychology* 151:331–349.

Cohen, Jeffrey J. 2017. "Drinking and Conferencing." *The Chronicle of Higher Education.* Retrieved October 4, 2019 (https://www.chronicle. com/article/DrinkingConferencing/240258).

Johnson, Paula A., Widnall, Shelia E., and Benya, Frazier F. 2018. *Sexual Harassment of Women: Climate, Culture, and Consequences in Academic Sciences, Engineering, and Medicine.* Washington, DC: The National Academies Press.

Lundsteen, Natalie. 2019. "When your Career Path Intersects with Alcohol." *Inside Higher Ed*. Retrieved October 6, 2019 (https://www.insidehighered.com/advice/2019/02/25/knowing-when-drink-alcohol-and-how-much-professional-events-opinion).

Miller, Allison. 2018. "In Some Disciplines, Heavy Drinking is Part of the Culture. That Can Be a Problem." *Science*. Retrieved October 4, 2019 (https://www.sciencemag.org/careers/2018/12/some-disciplines-heavy-drinking-part-culture-can-be-problem).

Nation, Maury, Crusto, Cindy, Wandersman, Abraham, Kumpfer, Karol L., Seybolt, Diana, Morrissey-Kane, Erin, and Davino, Katrina. 2003. "What Works in Prevention: Principles of Effective Prevention Programs." *American Psychologist* 58:449.

Richards, Tara N., Branch, Kathryn A., Fleury-Steiner, Ruth E., and Kafoneck, Katherine. 2017. "A Feminist Analysis of Campus Sexual Assault Policies: Results from a National Sample." *Family Relations* 66:104–115.

Sapiro, Virginia and Campbell, David. 2018. "Report on the 2017 APSA Survey on Sexual Harassment at Annual Meetings." *PS: Political Science and Politics* 51:197–206.

Shapiro, Deborah L. and Rinaldi, Alicia. (2001). "Achieving Successful Collaboration in the Evaluation of Sexual Assault Prevention Programs: A Case Study." *Violence Against Women* 7:1186–1201.

EIGHT

"They Tested with Stress": Solving Racial Injustice in Assessment by Acknowledging Adverse Childhood Experiences

Mawule A. Sevon and LaTrice L. Dowtin

In the 1990s, the late Tupac Shakur recorded the song "Ghetto Gospel," which encouraged listeners to consider the stress that continually confronted U.S. children living in impoverished environments due to racial and social injustices. The first part of the chapter title, "They Tested with Stress," is from the lyrics of that song, depicting the struggles of Black children. This theme is present throughout the chapter and is used to anchor the meaning of the chapter.

The Problem

Systemic racism in education is multifaceted, adversely affecting Black children. This social justice problem has three inseparable issues. There is the ignorance of adverse childhood experiences (ACEs) or trauma that disproportionality impact Black children throughout the U.S. This disproportionality is termed *pushout* to describe the discriminatory disciplinary and testing practices among Black children. The disregard of ACEs has schools using racially and culturally biased standardized tests, which promote misidentifying and inappropriately placing Black children in special education (SPED). Furthermore, school professionals' implicit racial and gender biases negatively impact Black children through harsh disciplinary practices that result in a higher number of Black children being suspended from school than children from other groups. Gender bias impacts the perception of Black girls differently than girls from other races. This bias, *adultification*, leads to the disproportionate punishment of Black girls. Black girls are viewed as being older, more knowledgeable about sexual interactions, needing less nurturance, more independent, and therefore deserving and capable of handling harsh punishments.

Many children experience ACEs, which is a fact that is neglected in educational policy. ACE exposure negatively impacts health and educational performance. According to Felitti and colleagues, researchers who published the original ACE study in 1998, ACEs are specific events occurring during childhood including family challenges (i.e., domestic violence, substance abuse, parental mental illness, parental separation, and parental incarceration), physical and emotional neglect, emotional, and physical and sexual abuse. While the impact of family challenges is well documented by researchers, practitioners and policymakers disregard their importance in considering developmental and academic growth.

Felitti and colleagues explored ACEs across ten categories; however, recent studies have found that Black children living in urban environments experience additional adversities. The Philadelphia Urban ACE study published in 2013 included adverse *neighborhood* experiences, racial discrimination, witnessing violence, bullying, and living in foster care. As considered in the Philadelphia Urban ACE study, the residual ramifications of centuries of racial discrimination are present because systematic racism continues to exist. While ACEs are not exclusive to Black children, Black children are at an increased disadvantage given unresolved historical oppression. From a policy perspective, little time is spent understanding the socioemotional needs of these students. The present system is more likely to refer a child for testing rather than examining the instructional practices in schools. However, placement in SPED does not equal an organic disability. Due to these biases against Black children and ignorance about the effects of ACEs, many schools do not provide safe learning environments for Black children.

Another social justice problem within education is the misuse of standardized assessments. The Every Student Succeeds Act continues to require the use of standardized testing to determine school accountability. Because federal law allows states to apply for local funding, schools are motivated to categorize underachieving students as having a disability. Educational policies enforce the use of statewide stakeholder tests and psychoeducational assessments to make decisions regarding school acceptance, grade level advancement, SPED placement, and achievement. This dangerous practice facilitates the disproportionality in SPED and generates negative outcomes throughout the lifespan.

The Research Evidence

Racial disparities in education have been well researched to cause problems such as discrepancies across academic performance, disciplinary responses, disproportionality in special education, increased entanglement in the criminal justice system, and underwhelming graduation rates. High-stakes and standardized assessments provide a funnel for pushing out Black students from the educational system. While data on student racial disparities can be interpreted to mean that Black children are low achievers, research has found that the standardized tests that are used to assess students are racially and culturally biased against students of color. Thus, the use of standardized testing is pushing out Black students. According to the U.S. Department of Education's *40th Annual Report to Congress on the Implementation of the Individuals with Disabilities Education Act, 2018*, Black students in elementary through secondary education are over two times more likely to be assigned an individualized education plan (IEP) for an emotional or intellectual disability compared to all the other racial and ethnic groups taken together. The racial disparities across the educational continuum are evident in additional national data sources. For example, the National Assessment for Education Progress Report Card for Reading found that in 2019 45 percent of White students in fourth grade performed at proficiency compared to only 15 percent of Black students. Similar results were reported for eighth graders.

Moreover, the pipeline from preschool to prison links student pushout to student involvement in the criminal justice system and impacts graduation rates. The U.S. Department of Education's Office for Civil Rights found that in the 2011–2012 school year, schools reported an estimated 92,000 school-based arrests. Similarly, in 2016, the U.S. Department of Education reported that Black preschoolers were 3.6 times more likely to receive one or more suspensions compared to White preschoolers. Alarmingly, Black children comprise 19 percent of preschool enrollment, while they make up 47 percent of preschool suspensions. According to data discussed in 2016 by researchers Meek and Gilliam, preschool suspension accurately predicts later suspension and expulsion. Preschoolers who are suspended are 10 times more likely to not graduate from high school and to become incarcerated than children who did not experience preschool suspension or expulsion.

ACE exposure can result in behaviors deemed by educators as challenging. In 2011, researchers Burke and colleagues examined the relationship between ACE exposure and learning and behavioral challenges. Results indicated that people with an ACE score of four or higher were 32 times more likely to present with a learning or behavioral problem compared to people with fewer ACEs. However, when these behaviors are displayed by Black children, they are more likely to be charged as behavioral problems than they are to be perceived as displaying trauma symptoms.

Gilliam and colleagues from Yale University Child Study Center (2016), using eye-tracking studies, found that problematic behaviors are often incorrectly identified and are observed more frequently in Black children. This highlighted a problem with implicit bias that negatively impacts Black boys. It is important to note that, while subsequent data will be discussed using gender binary language, it is understood that Black children of all genders experience these problems. When teachers were asked to identify students that they thought were displaying problem behaviors, 42 percent of teachers reported that the Black boys required the most attention. Therefore, they primarily found problem behaviors in Black children even though no actual problem behaviors existed. This shows that educators are more likely to accuse a Black child of displaying disruptive classroom behaviors even when the child presents with developmentally appropriate behaviors. This same study found that, even when educators are aware of the trauma history of a Black student, behaviors continue to be categorized as disruptive, warranting harsher punishments, and leading to unnecessary testing. This phenomenon of implicit bias harms the outcomes of Black children, such that they are more likely to have significant ACE exposure than children from other racial groups in urban communities. During the Philadelphia Urban ACE Survey in 2013, the Public Health Management Corporation examined race, income, and childhood adversity and found that Black people were more likely to report a detrimental rate (four or more) of adversity during childhood.

In 2017, Epstein and colleagues at Georgetown Law Center on Poverty and Inequality in "Girlhood Interrupted: The Erasure of Black Girls' Childhood" discussed the existence of and data surrounding adultification of Black girls. The Office for Civil Rights, U.S. Department of Education Civil Rights Data Collection "A First Look: Key Data Highlights on Equity & Opportunity Gaps in our Nation's Public Schools" (2016) found that Black girls made up only 8 percent of public school enrollment, but 13 percent of the out-of-school suspensions in the 2013–2014 school year. Furthermore, in 2014 the U.S. Department of Education for Civil Rights "Data

Snapshot" on school discipline reported that Black girls are suspended 12 percent more than most children, including all other girls and most boys.

In summary, the data outlines critical facts about the mistreatment of Black children throughout the educational system. Evidence highlights the facts that Black children are overcategorized in special education, are exceedingly punished, and are deemed as less deserving of sympathy and empathy compared to children of other cultures and races. Furthermore, while evidence shows that Black children are at higher risks for ACE exposure, current school practices are not aligned with research-based strategies that have efficacious outcomes for learners with childhood trauma. Finally, research illustrates that the existence of implicit bias is the underlying current that fuels these social injustices towards Black children.

Recommendations and Solutions

Policymakers, educators, and clinicians are uniquely positioned to evoke change and to provide support, advocacy, and alliance with this population when appropriately trained and knowledgeable on issues impacting Black children. This section provides concrete applicable solutions to the social justice problems of disproportionality of Black students in SPED, and of implicit racial and gender biases, and takes trauma-informed education to the next level.

1. Provide Implicit Bias Training to Individuals Enrolled in Educational Studies, and Train all School Staff and Faculty on Implicit Bias

Teachers and school administrators, directly and indirectly, impact the lives of students through policy creation, policy implementation, and general everyday interactions. At the foundation for changing the system to support and protect Black children is the need to understand the impact of implicit bias. Currently, many teacher and administrator training programs cover issues related to culture and diversity in one to two isolated courses. This practice can lead to educators being oblivious to the application of the pedagogical knowledge of diverse student populations because understanding implicit bias is fluid. Students and their behaviors are observed and measured using biased lenses. Psychoeducational assessments and standardized tests are often created by organizations and individuals who are unenlightened regarding the danger of implicit bias. In fact, all interactions and testing practices in education come with bias. One of the most common testing practices includes observation, which does not occur without bias when people are ill-trained in implicit biases. Recommendations for addressing these issues include:

- Embedding implicit bias training into teacher and administrator undergraduate- and graduate-level training programs. Every education course must include discussion and self-reflection on issues related to race and culture in post-secondary education.
- Requiring ongoing implicit bias training throughout the professional careers of all licensed and certified educators. The focus on implicit bias training must penetrate schools as an ongoing required process.
- Educators responsible for assessing behavioral concerns and designing and implementing interventions must have implicit bias training that is specific to their specialization.

2. Equip Teachers and School Administrators with ACE Scores of Students

When teachers and school administrators are equipped with aggregated ACE scores of the children in their schools (i.e., the number of children experiencing an abundance of trauma), they can reframe their thinking from *how do we fix these students?*, to *we can work to support the needs of these students*. A change in this thinking and changes to systemwide policies, can help close the achievement gap and decrease disproportionality within this population. Educators do not need to be privy to details of students' adversities. Having knowledge of whether students have an ACE score of four or higher provides enough information for educators to know when to implement trauma-sensitive approaches. To that effect, school resources can be dispersed to specific schools and classrooms when it is identified that many students with high ACE scores are clustered. The following is a recommendation for assessing adverse childhood experiences:

- School leadership should assess the ACE score of every child in their school.
  Examples of relevant tools include:
  - The Resilience Project
  - Center for Youth Wellness (CYW)
  - ACE Questionnaire (ACE-Q)

3. Provide Tier-Based Intervention Centered on the Known History of Trauma

Trauma-informed schools and classrooms create a learning environment where all students feel safe and nurtured, and their needs are met. Educational systems must provide evidence-based tiered interventions for students to reduce the use of ineffective and harmful disciplinary actions and over-testing of culturally diverse children. A tiered approach provides every student with basic levels of support while delivering additional resources to smaller groups of students based on their needs.

- Schools should utilize a tier-based intervention strategy to address ACEs. Listed next are the tiers of trauma-informed care which schools are recommended to incorporate.
  - Tier I: School-wide policies and procedures should be based on the knowledge of trauma's effect on the developing mind. Additionally, educators and school personnel must be trained to recognize the impact and signs of trauma exposure.
  - Tier II: Group interventions are utilized for students with suspected trauma exposure as a proactive approach to their unique needs. Consultation with school-based mental health clinicians provide teachers with evidence-based techniques for addressing classroom concerns
  - Tier III: Individual interventions treat trauma symptoms presenting in the classroom.

4. Require School-Based Mental Health Training for all Clinicians who Want to Work in Schools

Childhood mental health is critical. All children, including Black children, deserve qualified and well-trained mental health practitioners who are readily available in their schools. Mental health clinicians can be used to help support children through prevention and intervention efforts. Currently, many schools have school counselors and psychologists who have had limited or no training in school-based settings, which creates problems in their understanding and implementation of services in schools. Schools operate within and independently of other systems, thereby creating their own set of rules that govern them. Navigating school systems is often challenging for clinicians who were trained in other specialty areas such as in clinical and community settings. The time that it takes for non-school-based mental health practitioners to learn the intricacies of schools is vital time taken away from prevention and intervention services for Black children. Time is of the essence. This change in policy would help protect students by ensuring that highly trained school-based practitioners move forward to implement services that are specific to children in school settings without wasting children's resources or time. Here are some specific recommendations related to mental health clinicians working in schools:

- Qualifications for working in schools should be aligned with respective professional organizations and include mental health training.
- Clinicians who want to transition into school-based work must receive additional training and supervision in school counseling, school psychology, or school social work, depending on their field, to re-specialize in school-based settings.

5. Establish an Effective Student to School Psychologist Ratio

Schools throughout the nation have varied ratios for school psychologists. According to the National Association of School Psychologists (NASP), in 2015 there were roughly 1,381 students to each school psychologist. Often, schools in lower income areas have a larger and more harmful student to clinician ratio. These high ratios result in clinicians being overextended and engaged in reactive practices rather than proactive consultation and intervention implementation. School psychologists are trained to complete consultation with educational teams, and provide therapeutic services and support in the design of academic and behavioral interventions. Yet, due to their testing caseloads, they spend most of their time testing and identifying students for special education services. While NASP recommends a ratio of 500–700 students for each school psychologist, due to increased social disenfranchisement, discrimination, and poverty in urban communities which results in higher exposures to childhood adversities, schools within these communities would benefit from a lower student to mental health clinician ratio. A more effective ratio is outlined here:

- Create ratios based on the needs of the students and the community, which would be a maximum of 200–300 students to every school psychologist. This ratio would allow school psychologists ample time to build relationships with students and lead to decreases in child suicide, school violence, and bullying. Lastly, clinicians would increase their effectiveness when addressing the impact of community and national crises (e.g., mass shootings, deaths, or national unrest) on students and educational staff.

6. Conduct Appropriate Functional Behavior Assessments (FBA), and Design Practical and Appropriate Behavior Intervention Plans (BIP)

A functional behavior assessment is a measure used to determine the possible trigger, motivation, and impact of consequences on identified behaviors. Providers use the results of an FBA to design a BIP. A BIP provides a systematic and uniform method to decrease concerning behaviors and increase prosocial behaviors. Often, children with ACE exposure display behaviors determined by schools to be inappropriate or maladaptive, prompting referral for an FBA and BIP. However, the effectiveness of FBAs and BIPs are compromised because they frequently lack the details needed for complete teacher comprehension. It is impossible for teachers to utilize an FBA or a BIP that they do not understand. Furthermore, BIPs commonly include interventions that are impractical for classroom settings. While an FBA and a BIP can be useful in addressing concerning behaviors, the fact that they are routinely incorrectly implemented shows that they are unhelpful in their present form. Sometimes even the mention of the FBA and BIP process tends to generate increased teacher frustration. This frustration lends itself to the harsh punishments of students in urban schools and the use of unnecessary testing for these students. The following are methods of improving the utilization of FBAs and BIPs to improve the educational experiences of Black students:

- Train instructional staff on the utilization and application of FBAs and BIPs to ensure that educators are knowledgeable about the purposes they serve. Educators who have foundational knowledge about FBAs and BIPs would be comfortable requesting them.
- The FBA and BIP process must move toward a consultation model to allow school-based clinicians and teachers the opportunity to design, implement, and adjust the intervention collaboratively. This consultative process will create a fluid document that molds to the shifting needs of the student and the environment.

7. Allocate Funds to Support the Listed Resources

Implementing new policies without allocating suitable funding to sustain them is unacceptable. Funding allocation needs to be discussed early on in each school year. Opening this discussion early will allow for appropriate budgeting of all financial resources. Furthermore, this reallocation of money will reduce the high and ineffective cost of current special education spending by diverting efforts away from harmful resources and sending them towards culturally relevant and trauma-informed practices.

The present use of assessments and the racial injustices they produce are a social justice crisis, producing detrimental outcomes for Black students starting in preschool. Tupac Shakur brought attention to the impact of trauma on the next generation of Black children. Nearly three decades later, his lyrics and their intended message still ring true. As a result of historical racism and the lingering implications of oppression, Black students arrive in school with a lethal dosage of adversity. The same oppressive systems create implicit bias, allowing student stress to be disregarded and resulting in over-testing, exclusion, and misplacement into special education. This chapter presented a call for multilevel reform of the educational system due to the complexity of the presented problem. Eradicating social injustices in education for Black students will send them a message that we do not plan to leave them with an ill-fated world. Through the adoption of recommended solutions, Black children of the future will no longer be *tested with stress*.

Key Resources

Burke Harris, Nadine. 2018. *The Deepest Well: Healing the Long-Term Effects of Childhood Adversity.* New York, NY: Houghton Mifflin Harcourt.

Dowtin, LaTrice L. and Mawule A. Sevon. 2019. "The Black Panther Lives: Marveling at the Internal Working Models of Self in Young Black Children Through Play." Pp. 274–291 in *Using Superheroes and Villains in Counseling and Play Therapy: A Guide for Mental Health Professionals,* edited by L. Rubin. London: Routledge.

Felitti, Vincent J., Robert F. Anda, Dale Nordenberg, David F. Williamson, Alison M. Spitz, Valerie Edwards, Mary P. Koss, and James S. Marks. 1998. "The Relationship of Adult Health Status to Childhood Abuse and Household Dysfunction." *American Journal of Preventive Medicine* 14(4):245–258.

Gilliam, Walter S., Angela N. Maupin, Chin R. Reyes, Maria Accavitti, and Frederick Shic. 2016. "Do Early Educators' Implicit Biases Regarding Sex and Race Relate to Behavior Expectations and Recommendations of Preschool Expulsions and Suspensions. Research Study Brief." Paper presented at the U.S. Administration for Children and Families (ACF) 2016 State and Territory Administrators Meeting, September 28, Alexandria, VA.

Kramarczuk Voulgarides, Catherine, Edward Fergus, and Kathleen A. King Thorius. 2017. "Pursuing Equity: Disproportionality in Special Education and the Reframing of Technical Solutions to Address Systemic Inequities." *Review of Research in Education* 41(1):61–87.

Morris, Monique W. 2018. *Pushout: The Criminalization of Black Girls in Schools.* New York, NY: New Press.

Stevenson, Howard C. 2014. *Promoting Racial Literacy in Schools: Differences That Make a Difference.* New York, NY: Teachers College Press.

U.S. Department of Education. 2018. *40th Annual Report to Congress on the Implementation of the Individuals with Disabilities Education Act, 2018.* Washington, DC: Office of Special Education Programs.

NINE

Black Girls and School Suspension

Cherrell Green

The Problem

Rooted in the "tough on crime" rhetoric, stricter and more punitive discipline policies made their way into schools in the 1990s under the Clinton administration. The adoption of zero-tolerance policies (ZTP) was introduced following well-publicized violent incidents (e.g., Columbine), the perceived increases in violence in U.S. schools, and the passing of federal legislation (i.e., the Gun-Free Schools Act of 1994) that mandated schools to expel any student for at least one year for possessing a weapon on school grounds and provided financial incentives for schools who enacted ZTP. Formerly used to address the most egregious and problematic behaviors, the expansion of ZTP has led to the use of exclusionary discipline (e.g., suspension and expulsion) to punish students for violations of relatively minor behavior. Additionally, despite the promise of ZTP, research has generally found that ZTPs are largely ineffective and disproportionately punish Black students.

While the disproportionate suspension of Black males has been the focus of much contemporary scholarship, less attention has been devoted to the punishment of Black girls. This omission is particularly notable given that within the past decade, Black girls have experienced the fastest growing suspension rate among all students. As a result, an emerging body of research has begun to explore *why* Black girls are subject to disproportionate disciplinary practices. Scholars have found that, due to their marginalization at the nexus of both race and gender, Black girls are particularly vulnerable to experiencing inequitable treatment in schools.

The Research Evidence

Within the past decade Black girls have experienced the fastest growing suspension rate of all students; and nationally Black girls experience higher suspension rates than girls of different races and most boys of other races. According to the Department of Education Office of Civil Rights, in the 2015–2016 school year Black girls composed 8 percent of all students but were 14 percent of those suspended and 10 percent of students expelled, making them the *only* female racial/ethnic group to be disproportionately disciplined. These disparities in suspension begin as early as pre-school, where Black pre-school girls are suspended at a higher rate than any other group. In 2017, Black pre-school girls represented approximately 20 percent of the national female preschool enrollment population, but constituted 54 percent of female suspensions. While research has suggested that Black students experience higher rates of exclusionary discipline due to implicit stereotypes, Black girls are being disciplined for reasons that are distinct from their male peers. Researchers have suggested that Black girls are subject to both racial and gender stereotypes that place them at a higher risk of experiencing exclusionary discipline practices. In particular, racialized and gendered stereotypes about Black girls' sexuality, attitude, and aggressive nature is often used to criminalize behavior that does not confirm to traditional cultural standards of White femininity, which emphasize passivity, purity, and submissiveness. Thus, when Black girls exhibit behaviors that deviate or challenge these standards (e.g., independence, speaking up, or outwardly displaying anger), they are often subject to disciplinary sanctions. Subjective judgements of appropriate behavior are rooted in racial stereotypes and biases that can affect how student behavior is perceived and interpreted, ultimately undermining educational outcomes for Black girls.

These ideas receive some support in the research literature. When examining the intersections of race and gender simultaneously, scholars find that Black girls are often disciplined for less serious and subjective infractions labeled "disrespect," "willful defiance," "disobedience," and "insubordination." Due to stereotypes that characterize Black girls as loud, hostile, and aggressive, teachers often interpret Black girls' behaviors and communication style as disrespectful or unladylike. Consequently, Black girls are often reprimanded for failing to comply to gender-based expectations of behavior that encourage traditional standards for femininity (e.g. docility).

In a study of a single school district in Colorado during the 2011–2012 school year, researchers found that Black girls were 53 percent more likely than White and Hispanic girls to receive an office referral for behaviors labeled as disobedience and defiance. Additionally, they also found when Black and White girls were referred to the office for the *same* behaviors as other female students, Black girls were more likely to be punished more severely. In another study, of a single Midwestern school district, the authors found that Black girls were more likely to be disciplined than White and Hispanic female students for behaviors labeled as defiance or physical aggression. In a more recent rigorous study, examining disciplinary records of White, Black, Hispanic, and Asian male and female students in grades 6–12, scholars found that Black girls were still more likely to receive an office referral for less serious and subjective offenses.

Additionally, Black girls are also disciplined for wearing certain hair styles such as braids and locs, or even their naturally textured hair such as afros. In some school districts, the wearing of cultural items such as head wraps and scarves, except for religious purposes, is also grounds for suspension. Racial and gendered stereotypes often view these cultural displays of Blackness as "inappropriate" or "unprofessional." Relatedly, dress-code violations are another way racial and gender biases impact Black girls. Highly subjective language in dress-code policies make it easier for school administrators to police Black girls' bodies. This is often based on stereotypes that characterize Black girls as hypersexual and less feminine than girls of other races.

Qualitative studies have also explored how race and gender influence disciplinary practices for Black girls. In a two-year ethnographic study of a middle school, research has found that Black girls were more likely to be admonished for not comporting traditional cultural standards of femininity than White and Hispanic girls. Specifically, Black girls who were perceived as behaving in ways that were synonymous with stereotypical images of Black women as loud and defiant were viewed by school administrators as needing greater social control or correction in the form of school discipline. In classrooms, many teachers interpret Black girls' speaking up and asking questions as inappropriate and assertive, as traditional femininity standards encourage docility. What would be considered inquisitive behavior, behavior often encouraged among students, is perceived as "too assertive," "too aggressive," "too loud," and combative. In a qualitative study that explored the discipline experiences of seven persistently disciplined middle school girls, scholars found that Black girls felt that they were unsupported by educators – a result of misinterpretations of Black girls' behavior.

Teachers' failure to understand behaviors and cultural differences among Black female students often led to greater use of exclusionary punishment and Black girls feeling disconnected from school.

Recommendations and Solutions

Scholars suggest that the overreliance on school disciplinary practices for Black girls is, in part, due to implicit biases that exacerbate stereotypes about Black femininity and punish Black girls for failure to comport with traditional gender expectations. Consequently, for Black girls who have been subject to these practices, these assumptions have led to greater short- and long-term outcomes such as dropping out of school, contact with the juvenile and criminal justice system, and unemployment. Given their vulnerability, it is imperative to identify potential strategies that could reduce disparate treatment for Black girls.

Research

- There is a need to fund and support data collection efforts that document the use of disciplinary practices in schools. Particularly efforts should be focused on documenting the types of infractions and disaggregation based on race and sex. Furthermore, this is data should be collected in a timely fashion and be made publicly available. It is critical that researchers have access to this data as they can more fully explore how intersections of race and gender can contribute to disproportionate punishment of Black girls in schools. In doing so, researchers would be able to identify disparities, track progress, and evaluate interventions or policies.
- Additionally, while research consistently finds that Black girls are often chastised for speaking up or being "too loud," more research is needed to explore *why* Black girls may be speaking up in classrooms. Black girls speaking up may be a response to perceived inequitable treatment in schools.

Laws and Policies

- Steps should be taken to change or repeal laws that contribute to the disproportionality of Black girls in school discipline. Some changes can occur at the local level as school districts have extensive control over their codes of conduct (COC) and the application of appropriate disciplinary responses.

- When administrators or legislators are developing or interpreting existing policies, they should include the voices and perspectives of Black girls. Including Black girls in the development of policy has several positive benefits. By including Black girls in policymaking decisions, any potential biases in existing policies that may otherwise go undetected can be addressed. Secondly, they can share their perspectives and experiences with school disciplinary practices and address negative stereotypes that have been imposed on their behaviors. This allows Black girls' voices to be heard, without having their speaking up being misinterpreted as "acting out." Lastly, if Black girls are included in policymaking decisions, they can use their own agency in their education to become civically engaged and advocate for policies that disproportionately affect Black girls.

Administration

- Educational administrators (e.g., superintendents, principals etc.) should regularly conduct equity audits to ensure that schools are collecting accurate disciplinary data and to assess whether disciplinary practices are administered fairly within schools and school districts.
- Relatedly, given that research has found that a small number of classroom teachers contribute to a substantial number of disciplinary referrals, it is crucial that educational administrators prioritize working with educators on appropriate classroom management skills. This is especially important as Black girls are often disciplined for subjective infractions (e.g., disrespect, defiance).
- Administrators need to create a culture within their districts, schools, and classrooms that does not heavily rely on the use of exclusionary punishment but encourages a culture that promotes a supportive and nurturing learning environment for *all students*. This would include providing some of the following interventions: school-wide implicit bias trainings and culturally competent professionals to provide counseling and mental health services – for both educators and students.

Educators

- Instead of relying on disciplinary practices, educators should receive *ongoing* cultural competency training. This training should provide educators with an in-depth understanding of historical and contemporary racism, but also of the subtle covert ways in which institutions, laws, and policies serve to reinforce inequality. This training would also be able to provide educators with an opportunity to understand the linguistic differences in how Black girls communicate as this would significantly reduce the dissension in the classroom between educators and students and the misinterpretation of behaviors. Importantly, if feasible, it would be best that these trainings begin in early teaching training programs – or even before student teachers obtain their certification.

• Additionally, educators should receive implicit bias training that addresses their own stereotypes and biases they hold about Black girls, which ultimately influences their disciplinary practices.

Programs

• Educational programs or interventions that take an exclusively race– or gender-centered approach fall short of truly understanding how race and gender work simultaneously to disproportionately affect Black girls. For example, positive behavior intervention and support (PBIS) programs have demonstrated some effectiveness in reducing disciplinary disparities. However, often absent in these approaches is an *explicit* focus on race and gender to address the needs of Black girls. Future interventions need to adapt interventions such as PBS with culturally competent and gender-responsive approaches.

• Programs and interventions should be not only culturally responsive and gender informed, but also trauma informed. Black girls – some of whom are victims of trauma, are often characterized as aggressors and disciplined for "acting out." Trauma-informed and trauma-responsive practices are critical in addressing the underlying issues that contribute to Black girls' misbehavior. Leaving trauma unaddressed only pushes Black girls further out of school and into the hands of the juvenile justice system.

Black girls are often excluded from the national discourse concerning school disciplinary practices. This is a grave misstep as Black girls are being disciplined at disproportionate rates relative to other students due to their intersecting gendered and racialized identities. Unfortunately subject to scrutiny and implicit bias, Black girls struggle to navigate two marginalized identities that characterize them as less innocent, unfeminine, and undeserving of equitable treatment. It is of utmost importance that researchers, educators, and policymakers come together to give primacy to research that focuses on Black girls' educational experiences; enact and eradicate legislation that disproportionately affects Black girls; and implement gender-responsive, trauma-responsive and culturally informed interventions and strategies to reduce disciplinary disparities and more importantly, improve educational outcomes for Black girls.

Key Resources

Annamma, Subini, Yolanda Anyon, Nicole M. Joseph, Jordan Farrar, Eldridge Greer, Barbara Downing, and John Simmons. 2019. "Black Girls and School Discipline: The Complexities of Being Overrepresented and Understudied." *Urban Education* 54: 211–242.

Blake, Jamila J., Bettie Ray Butler, Chance W. Lewis, and Alicia Darensbourg. 2011. "Unmasking the Inequitable Discipline Experiences of Urban Black Girls: Implications for Urban Educational Stakeholders." *Urban Review* 43: 90–106.

Epstein, Rebecca, Jamilia J. Blake, and Thalia Gonzalez. 2017. *Girlhood Interrupted: The Erasure of Black Girls' Childhood*. Georgetown Law Center on Poverty and Inequality. Retrieved from https://www.law.georgetown.edu/poverty-inequality-center/wp-content/uploads/sites/14/2017/08/girlhood-interrupted.pdf.

George, Janel A. 2015. "Stereotype and School Pushout: Race, Gender, and Discipline Disparities." *Arkansas Law Review* 68: 101–129.

Morris, Edward W. 2007. "Ladies or Loudies? Perceptions and Experiences of Black Girls in Classrooms." *Youth & Society* 38: 490–515.

Morris, Edward W., and Brea L. Perry. 2017. "Girls Behaving Badly? Race, Gender, and Subjective Evaluation in the Discipline of African-American Girls." *Sociology of Education* 90: 127–148.

Morris, Monique W. 2016. *Pushout: The Criminalization of Black Girls in Schools*. New York, NY: The New Press.

Skiba, Russell J., Robert S. Michael, Abra Carroll Nardo, and Reece L. Peterson. 2002. "The Color of Discipline: Sources of Racial and Gender Disproportionality in School Punishment." *The Urban Review* 34: 317–342.

U.S. Department of Education Office for Civil Rights. 2014. *Civil Rights Data Collection. Data Snapshot: School Discipline*. Retrieved from https://www2.ed.gov/about/offices/list/ocr/docs/crdc-discipline-snapshot.pdf.

SECTION IV

Crime and (In)Justice

TEN

Police Homicides: The Terror of "American Exceptionalism"

Robert Aponte and Hannah Hurrle

The Problem

Police-on-civilian homicides have become a critical social issue in the US in recent years due to newly emerging information on the parameters of the problem and the often egregiousness of the killings. Key to the heightened attention is the increasingly widespread recording and sharing of these gruesome killings via cell-phone cameras, social media, and police cameras. Particularly disturbing is the virtual impunity from sanctions accorded nearly all such shooters, along with the startling frequency of the shootings in the US, as compared with other advanced societies.

Over 1,000 persons have been killed by police annually in the US in recent years, with nearly all shot to death, and the remainder tasered, beaten, or otherwise slain. In the first 24 days of 2015, 59 persons were killed by police in the US, whereas only 55 persons were correspondingly slain in the UK in the last 24 years. Similar imbalances exist compared with other advanced nations (e.g., Germany, Japan, Canada, France, and Denmark) in both absolute and relative numbers. While a proportion of the US shootings may have been justified (e.g., suspects pointed weapons or shot at police), most involved lesser provocations and the vast majority could have been avoided if the developing de-escalation techniques had been employed.

Although more Whites than Blacks are slain by police, the role of racism in the killings of many Blacks is evident from their substantially disproportionate numbers, and from the comparatively trivial nature of their provocations. Overall, Blacks are between two and three times as likely to be killed than Whites. Latinos/Native Americans are also disproportionately slain, though at lower rates than Blacks. But, the problem goes well beyond racism. Non-Hispanic Whites in the US are still 26 times as likely to be killed by police than citizens in Germany of any race or racial background. The greater probability of Whites getting shot in the US is consistent with data on police shootings in other advanced nations – civilians are far more likely to be shot in the US.

The killings in the US are also related to an array of factors, uniquely American, which facilitate the carnage and undermine accountability. For one, the US is the only nation where there are more guns than people. This amount of firepower makes police more fearful, thereby eliciting defensive aggressiveness. Worse, major lethal military hardware (tanks, etc.) have been distributed to police agencies, which foster even more violence. There is the code of silence (police feeling that they cannot inform on colleagues), limited immunity (laws/union contracts providing rights to police under fire for shootings, etc., thereby stifling investigations), training highly skewed toward violence, and the enormous deference accorded to police, especially by prosecutors – who often enjoy collegial relations with police and are often reluctant to prosecute even the most egregious killings. Rather, "justice" is provided via major lawsuit payouts – millions yearly. Yet, even in the payouts, many of the entitled are shortchanged.

The Research Evidence

Until recently, few sources of reliable police shooting data were available. Fortunately, led by "The Counted," a series in the British progressive daily, the *Guardian*, followed by the *Washington Post*'s own series, solid data are now available, although primarily for 2015–2018. The federal government is reportedly constructing such a data set, but none has yet emerged.

Current (2019) estimates of the disproportionate killings of Blacks over Whites are 2.5 killings of Blacks for every killing of Whites. Blacks are also twice as likely as Whites to be slain while unarmed. Under the largely abandoned 'stop and frisk' policies, Blacks and Latinos were far more frequently detained, but far less likely to be carrying contraband. In Chicago, ethnographic work in courtrooms found many police, judges, and attorneys engaging in virulent racist talk. That city's police killed 92 civilians between 2010 and 2015, 80 percent of whom were Black, though Blacks comprised only 30 percent of the city's population. From another angle, Harvard researchers found that police-inflicted injuries on civilians across the country, measured by emergency room visits between 2001 and 2014, revealed a Black victimization rate 4.9 times that of Whites'. More recently, evidence of police racism surfaced when thousands of racist memes originating from police officers throughout the country were found on social media. Philadelphia, for example, has moved to fire 13 officers for the offenses, with other cities poised to follow.

Guns are widely seen by experts as the most salient single factor in the rates of police killings in the US, compared with other advance nations. The US is the most armed society on earth – the only one to contain more guns than people. National surveys have long produced data on gun ownership by household and state or region. Harvard researchers have shown that where gun ownership is high, police kill more civilians than in low ownership areas. For example, in the high-ownership states of Alabama, Georgia, Idaho, Kentucky, and Louisiana, there were an astounding 3.6 times as many lethal shootings by police than in such low-ownership states as Connecticut, Hawaii, and Massachusetts. Correspondingly, civilian killings of police were 3.0 times as numerous in the high-ownership areas. Consequently, despite typically conservative leanings, many police organizations oppose liberal gun-ownership laws.

The code of silence is a long known strategy among police to shield wrong-doing from scrutiny, whereby fellow officers must never report misbehavior by colleagues. Numerous police have testified to its widespread influence, including Frank Serpico of the NYPD, whose exploits were popularized in a film bearing his name. Violations of the norm can bring repercussions from ostracism to abandonment in dangerous circumstances. A recent survey of nearly 1,000 randomly selected police from 121 agencies found that over half agreed that police often turn a blind eye to wrongdoing by colleagues. Over 60 percent even disagreed with the idea that police always report *serious criminal* violations. Relatedly, the long established expression "testilying" denotes the not uncommon practice of lying in court to avoid providing damaging evidence. Regarding retaliation, two Chicago police officers helped the FBI bring down a rogue colleague and, in the aftermath, were so badly treated by their colleagues that they sued and won a $2 million award. The increase in recordings of these incidents has uncovered wrongdoing that would previously have been shielded by code-inspired dishonesty.

There is also virtual immunity from accountability. Despite thousands of killings from 2005 to 2015, only 54 officers were charged for any of killings. A variety of factors facilitated this. Records clearly show that juries are reluctant to convict police officers and that prosecutors are slow to charge them. Generally, those charged had been video-recorded, shot unarmed suspects in the back, or, in rare instances, had other police testify against them. Still, most of the defendants were acquitted, had the charges dropped, or faced reduced charges, sometimes leading to clean criminal records. Among those fired, many were rehired by other police agencies. Whatever the outcome, the individual shooters are never required to pay fees for court costs, lawsuits, etc.

Laws and, especially, police union contracts provide enormous protections to police under investigation. In Maryland, police who have killed are allowed 10 days before they are required to speak with investigators; 13 other states have similar laws. Union contracts mandate similar provisions in other areas. Reuters' investigation of 82 police union contracts found that police disciplinary records were routinely erased after periods ranging from 6 months to 3 years. Half of the contracts allowed for the accused officers to view all forms of evidence against them prior to providing their account of the incident. Complaints were often time-limited, and were seldom sustained. Of 1,000 complaints lodged in Chicago in 2016, only one resulted in a disciplinary finding.

Efforts to modify such protections are fiercely fought by the unions. While police have to be certified (essentially, licensed), decertifying police is difficult, even when they face substantial disciplinary action. Those actually decertified in one area can typically reenter law enforcement in another area. Efforts to establish a registry of decertified officers over several decades have languished due to union pressures.

Typically, shootings result in lawsuit payouts, as the sole form of "justice" or "accountability" that is available to survivors. For example, between 2004 and 2014, Chicago expended some $521 million in payouts. Between 2011 and 2014, New York paid out some $348 million, and $101 million was paid by Los Angeles from 2002 to 2011. Other cities have also paid out millions.

Standard police training strongly overemphasizes techniques of violence and begets fear and readiness to strike. Recruitment videos often feature shoot-outs, SWAT teams, and militarized equipment. After years of excess military hardware being distributed to police agencies, research determined that possession of the weaponry alone furthered police violence. In addition, a national police agency revealed that police typically receive only 8 hours of de-escalation training, but over 100 hours of training in firearms and fighting techniques. By contrast, European police are trained to use violence as a last resort. They spend far more time on de-escalation training, and they conform to the European Convention on Human Rights. This standard holds that violence can be used only when "absolutely necessary." This contrasts with the US standard which allows for violence when officers have a "reasonable belief" that suspects pose a threat.

Recommendations and Solutions

Policy options to deal with the problem face numerous obstacles, beyond the complexity of the issues alone. For example, the vast majority of shooters are neither state nor federal officers; they are local police. Not only do the states have their own laws on these issues, but the hundreds of thousands of jurisdictions employing the shooters also have varying rules and guidelines, and typically they are not well funded. In the largest cities, where the heart of the problem lies, police unions are often extremely powerful, protective of their membership, and resentful of reforms. Overall, judges, juries, and prosecutors are typically very pro-police and many are overtly racist.

The multiplicity of police agencies, estimated at 18,000 strong, is a serious obstacle to reform. Most other western nations have national systems, which extend to budgetary items, rather than having hundreds of autonomous agencies scattered throughout the country. National systems allow for easy implementation of national standards on police practices, unlike the case in the US. But the financing factor is also quite serious. To raise capital, strapped agencies, like that in Ferguson, Missouri, where major civil disturbances occurred after a questionable shooting, often turn to issuing large-scale summonses, even for the most minor infractions. These campaigns poison police–community relations. Standards for hiring or retaining police are also undermined under the fiscal constraints. Many of the police officers charged in shootings, for example, should never have been hired due to their existing checkered pasts. Clearly, the need for adequate distribution of resources across police agencies is substantial and the shortfall contributes to the carnage. There are certain policies that are needed:

1. A national standard: First off, it is clear that a national policy must be established stating the conditions in which police officers may shoot at suspects legally. Such a proposal was introduced by a congressman as early as 2000, though it never passed. This cannot wait. All experts agree on the keen need for such a policy. California recently adopted the first such policy in the nation. From January 2020, California police are no longer permitted to use deadly force when circumstances make a shooting seem "reasonable." Rather, they will be permitted to shoot only when "necessary." Such a policy may retain a measure of subjectivity, but it is a necessary step in the right direction.

2. Training in de-escalation: Clearly among the major prevailing topics in the profession is de-escalation. Increasingly popular, the

technique has had positive results for many agencies that have tried it. Worries that de-escalation might endanger police officers have not been borne out. Implementing a national mandate to increase de-escalation training is imperative.

3. Special prosecutors: Every police shooting case should be assigned a special prosecutor. This would counteract the biases of local district attorneys who have to prosecute police officers with whom they have friendly relations. The extra expenses could be borne by the federal government. Local prosecutors are unlikely to object, since this reform would reduce the inevitable conflicts produced by their loyalty to the police and their commitment to professional standards. Police unions might well object, but it would be difficult for them to argue that only local prosecutors should oversee indictments of their members.

4. The code of silence must be broken. Hotlines for providing anonymous tips, monetary rewards, and positive recognition for those willing to speak up, and real penalties for police perjury, would all help enormously. Though some would resist such measures, few would argue publicly that the code somehow serves the public good. In fact, many police officers would welcome the alleviation it would offer them, since fear of retaliation is the key reason they cooperate with the code.

5. Transparency (more than just cameras): Police cameras must be made available to all police agencies and their use nationally mandated. While they are not foolproof, they have repeatedly provided clarity to contentious descriptions of police–civilian encounters. Footage must also be made public if they are to serve their purpose. Just as urgent is the necessity of a federal mandate stopping police from interfering with civilians recording police–civilian encounters, save where the civilian is truly interfering with the police action.

6. Shooting in cars: Shooting at people in cars who are not clearly endangering anyone should be forbidden. As far back as 1972, New York police banned this practice. In the near half century since the ban, no police officer has ever been seriously hurt by someone in a car. Yet, many innocent passengers have been maimed or killed by police shooting at cars. Many agencies still allow this unjustified practice. It must be stopped.

7. SWAT and militarization: The militarization of the police needs to be reversed. Evidence shows that the war-like weaponry underlying militarization, provided by the federal government, fosters violence, while there are no cases in which the military hardware has saved lives. SWAT raids were initially created for

rare, hostage-holding situations. But, over time, they have been used almost exclusively in drug raids, which typically yield little of law enforcement value. They frequently yield only small stashes of drugs and low level dealers. Many innocents have been needlessly slain in such raids and police officers have occasionally been killed in them. SWAT team raids should either be banned or be severely curtailed and well regulated.

8. Reporting gun drawings: In recent research, it was found that in police departments that have officers report each time they draw their guns, but do not shoot, police–civilian killings were lower than elsewhere. The policy was reportedly well accepted. Hence, it should be mandated.

9. Lone police: Police who encounter suspects while working alone should be required to call for reinforcements or for advice from senior officers before advancing on a suspect. Overall, about half of the shootings target suspects holding guns, but only about one third of lone-officer shootings involve suspects holding guns. Moreover, killings by lone officers are four times as likely to involve unarmed suspects as when officers are grouped. This is a serious overrepresentation and warrants mandating the policy.

10. Other circumstances: When a suspect has no weapon, shootings should be prohibited. At least 100 unnecessary killings in 2015 involved such unarmed suspects. Likewise, suspects armed with weapons other than guns should not be shot. These weapons have little potential for killing police except when the suspect and the officer are in very close proximity. Finally, suspects fleeing on foot should not be shot unless there is credible evidence that the suspect will kill or assault if not stopped.

Conclusion

The problem of police shootings is complex and a wide variety of policy shifts will be necessary to reduce the carnage. A number of recommendations suggested here have been tried and show signs of change and success. Most importantly, de-escalation techniques have been increasingly adopted by police departments, including those of Camden (NJ), Chicago (IL), Dallas (TX), Denver (CO), Los Angeles (CA), Minneapolis (MN), New York City (NY) and Salt Lake City (UT). Dallas, for example, experienced a drop of nearly 20 percent in use-of-force incidents after implementing de-escalation. Salt Lake City went two years without a single shooting after they began their program, and excessive force complaints fell from 65 to 15 in three years after

Camden began their version. Other reforms being tried may also be having a positive impact. In fact, if the current trend holds, preliminary figures suggest that 2019 may produce at least 80–85 fewer police-on-civilian shooting deaths than 2018, a significant and welcome decrease.

Key Resources

Chabria, Anita. 2019. Newsom signs "Stephon Clark's Law" setting new rules on police use of force. Sacramento, California. *Los Angeles Times.* Retrieved November 1, 2019 (https://www.latimes.com/politics/la-pol-ca-california-police-use-of-force-law-signed-20190711-story.html).

Hemenway, David, Deborah Azrael, Andrew Conner, and Matthew Miller. 2019. Variation in rates of fatal police shootings across US States: The role of firearm availability. *Journal of Urban Health* 96(1): 63–73.

Jennings, Jay and Meghan E. Rubado. 2017. Preventing the use of deadly force: The relationship between police agency policies and rates of officer involved gun deaths. *Public Administration Review* 77(2): 217–226.

Lockhart, P.R. 2019. Police posted thousands of offensive memes on Facebook. Now some of them are being fired. *Vox Media.* Retrieved November 1, 2019 (https://www.vox.com/identities/2019/7/19/20701048/police-officer-facebook-racism-philadelphia-plain-view-project).

Lott, Joshua. 2018. $16 Million vs. $4: In fatal police shootings, payouts vary widely. *New York Times.* Retrieved November 1, 2019 (https://www.nytimes.com/2018/06/28/us/police-shootings-payouts.html).

President's Task Force on 21st Century Policing. 2015. *Final Report of the President's Task Force on 21st Century Policing.* Washington, DC: Office of Community Oriented Policing Services.

Swedler David, Molly Simmons, Francesca Dominici, and David Hemenway. 2015. Firearm prevalence and homicides of law enforcement officers in the United States. *American Journal of Public Health* 105(10): 2042–2048.

The Marshall Project. 2019 *Police Settlements: A Curated Collection of Links.* New York. Retrieved November 1, 2019 (https://www.themarshallproject.org/records/1712-police-settlements).

Van Cleve, Nicole Gonzalez. 2016. *Crook County: Racism and Injustice in America's Largest Criminal Court.* Stanford, CA: Stanford University Press.

Zimring, Franklin. 2017. *When Police Kill.* Cambridge, MA: Harvard University Press.

ELEVEN

Crimmigration: The Presumption of Illegality and the Criminalization of Immigrants

Kristen M. Budd and Bianca E. Bersani

The Problem

Throughout U.S. history, rising waves of immigration have given way to rising waves of angst over immigrant crime. Today, nearly half of all Americans believe immigration makes crime worse for the U.S. With current estimates predicting immigrants will drive U.S. population growth, accounting for 88 percent of the population increase between 2015 and 2065, growing trepidation and alarm regarding immigrants is not only probable, but also problematic. Whereas immigration has been at the top of political agendas for numerous administrations, the relationship between immigration and crime is at the forefront of current political and public discourse. Today's rhetoric reinforces the notion that (more) immigration increases the rate of crime and this social discourse is exacerbated by media depictions of the criminal-immigrant. The social construction of the criminal-immigrant persists despite a hearty scientific basis demonstrating immigrants have relatively low levels of criminal involvement even with exposure to traditional criminogenic risk factors (e.g., instability, residence in disadvantaged areas) and at a time when the apprehension of criminal undocumented immigrants at the border continue to decline to historically low levels.

Looking back, these waves of angst and corresponding discourse and rhetoric, brought about a socio-legal response to the alleged criminal-immigrant, "crimmigration," a term coined by legal scholar Julie Stumpf in her 2006 publication "The Crimmigration Crisis: Immigrants, Crime, and Sovereign Power." Starting in the 1980s, and persisting today, crimmigration has been demarcated by a disappearing delineation between (civil) immigration law and criminal law. Through a series of sometimes-incremental changes to laws and their enforcement, these two traditionally separate areas of law – immigration and criminal – have become intertwined. This fusion of law not only influences policies and practices throughout the criminal justice system, but also the framing of an important social and human rights issue. As a result, we have a social milieu characterized by the presumption of illegality and the criminalization of a class of people.

While such narratives have the power to skew public perceptions of immigrant criminality, the effect is more pervasive, shaping local, state, and federal decisions regarding formal responses to immigration and crime and the allocation of scarce public safety resources. These formal responses to the socially constructed criminal-immigrant include law enforcement practices as well as wider justice system practices. To illustrate, law enforcement has been militarized at the border with federal directives to separate families attempting to enter the U.S., and local-level police sharing responsibility for enforcing immigration laws – officially a federal enforcement responsibility. Traditionally adjudicated in immigration courts as civil offenses, immigration-related offenses that are subject to criminal prosecution have expanded in number, and simultaneously many misdemeanor offenses have been deemed deportable offenses, and federal dockets are most commonly prosecuting immigration-related offenses. Within the court system immigrants experience a form of double punishment, as they are subject to both criminal (e.g., imprisonment) and immigration (e.g., detention, deportation) sanctions. Crimmigration plays out in the correctional system with the increased use of private prisons to confine and detain individuals presumed to have committed and with known immigration offenses. These socio-legal responses only further serve to reinforce the mythic narrative of the criminal-immigrant, which mounting scientific evidence continues to debunk.

The Research Evidence

The Immigrant–Non-Criminal Nexus

- A National Academies of Sciences (2015) review of the research reveals a common pattern whereby, compared to U.S.-born individuals, immigrants are far less likely to commit crime regardless of country of birth or type of crime. According to a study conducted by Bersani and colleagues (2018), published in the journal *Migration*

Letters, undocumented individuals are less likely to commit crime compared to their documented immigrant and U.S.-born peers. This finding aligns with research conducted by the CATO Institute, a public policy research organization, that finds lower incarceration and conviction rates for undocumented immigrants compared with their documented and U.S.-born peers.

- Ousey and Kubrin's (2018) recent meta-analysis documents communities with a high concentration of immigrants have lower crime rates compared to those with a lower concentration. As the concentration of immigrants in a community increases, rates of crime in the same community decrease. Research conducted by Light and Miller (2018), published in the journal *Criminology*, find increased concentrations of undocumented immigrants at the state level are linked to declines in rates of violent crime.

- Mounting evidence from published studies such as those conducted by Lyons, Vélez, and Santoro (2013) in the *American Sociological Review*, Martínez-Schuldt and Martínez (2019) in *Justice Quarterly*, and O'Brien, Collingwood, and El-Khatib (2019) in *Urban Affairs Review* find the adoption of sanctuary policies does not increase crime and has instead been linked with declines in crime and increases in reporting of crime victimization to authorities.

- According to national-level data (e.g., the Federal Bureau of Investigation's Uniform Crime Reports), despite large increases in the immigrant population over the last two decades, crime rates generally and violent crimes rates specifically have continued to decline.

- According to U.S. Department of Justice data for the fiscal year 2018, while 64 percent of federal arrests were of non-citizens, the majority were immigrant-related arrests, not arrests for drug trafficking or violent crimes.

The Dispersion of Immigration Enforcement and the Justice System

- Legislation efforts have redistributed responsibility for immigrant identification, law enforcement, and confinement from the federal level to the local level. Section 287(g) of the Immigration and Nationality Act allows the Department of Homeland Security to deputize state- and local-level police to perform immigration enforcement functions.

- The dispersion of immigrant enforcement has resulted in a patchwork of policing efforts nationally and within states. According to the National Conference of State Legislatures' 2017 Immigration Report, certain states, like Arizona, *require* law enforcement agencies to check the immigration status of all individuals they encounter. In contrast, California law *prohibits* state and local law enforcement agencies from using money or personnel to investigate or arrest persons for immigration enforcement purposes.

- According to research conducted by Armenta (2017) in the journal *Sociology of Race and Ethnicity*, Beckett and Evans (2015) in the journal *Law & Society Review*, Davies and Fagan (2012) in *The ANNALS of the American Academy of Political and Social Science*, and Reid and colleagues (2005) in *Social Science Research*, immigrants and immigrant communities are subject to heightened policing and sanctions such as pre-trial detention compared to non-immigrants with the same charge(s).
- Beginning in 1965, the Immigration and Nationality Act made illegal entry a misdemeanor offense, rather than a civil offense, with the focus directed at detaining and deporting serious or violent offenders. By 1980, immigration offenses were consequent to increasingly severe charges.
- Immigrants have a right to retained council, but are not guaranteed council by the Sixth Amendment. A report by the American Immigration Council reveals only 37 percent of all immigrants and 14 percent of those detained pre-trial secured legal representation in removal cases. Representation is decisive, with represented immigrants significantly more successful in obtaining immigration relief.
- While private prisons have been documented as the sites of a wide range of human rights abuses, they are benefitting from the current administration's goal to expand the detention capacity of migrants to up to 80,000 immigrants per day. According to the National Immigrant Justice Center's November 2017 data, 71 percent of the average daily-detained immigration population were held in privately owned jails (roughly 15,000 people per day across 33 jails).
- In the fiscal year 2017, the Department of Homeland Security reports the majority of individuals removed from the U.S. were non-criminal.

Recommendations and Solutions

The presumption of illegality has led to the criminalization of a group of people based on their place of birth rather than the behaviors they engage in. Consequently, controlling crime has become inextricably linked with migration to the U.S. At the federal, state, and local levels, this fusion of civil law and criminal law (i.e., crimmigration law), policing practices, and criminal justice-led responses has led the criminalization of immigrants. The recommendations and solutions that follow provide a framework to begin to disentangle the complex socio-legal relationship between immigration and criminality, with particular focus on law and criminal justice responses to immigrants. In addition, we propose recommendations to dispel the myth of the criminal immigrant and to also further our understanding of immigrants, assimilation, and criminality.

1. Immigration, Law, and Policy

- We recommend the termination of any laws or policies – whether they are at the federal, state, or local level – that target racial and ethnic minorities to assess immigration status. These types of laws and policies can lead to racial profiling and the erosion of trust in social institutions meant to promote prosocial community ties and public safety.
- Families should be kept together. There should be an end to harmful immigration practices, such as the separation of families (at the border; work raids). Family separation and mass deportation strategies penalize not only the deported individual - the vast majority of whom are non-criminal - but also their children, significant other, and community. One key ramification is the deterioration of factors known to reduce the likelihood of offending including strong bonds to family and school. Consequently, the continued advancement of mass deportation strategies that disrupt families and communities are likely to backfire and produce the very thing they seek to control – crime.
- Grant legal status to immigrants who entered the U.S. without documentation as children. According to a recent 2018 public opinion conducted by the Pew Research Center, a nonpartisan fact tank, 73 percent of U.S. adults favor granting legal status to children who were unlawfully brought to the U.S. While partisan divides exist, the majority of respondents identifying as Republican (54 percent) and Democratic (89 percent) support this policy proposal.
- Improve pathways to legal entry and legal status using humane and fair treatment. One critical need is the simplification of the asylum process. Seeking asylum is a human right and should not be denied to those who have a history of persecution or fear of persecution upon returning to their home country. Attorneys, language services, and resources should be directed to assist this legal pathway to residency and alleviate the extensive backlog of cases. With the signing of the Protocol Relating to the Status of Refugees in 1967, the U.S. is legally obligated to protect those who qualify as refugees. Current

efforts aimed at drastically reducing pathways to asylum and refugee status run counter to this treaty.

- Increase accessibility to known factors that suppress crime and promote integration: preserving family units, pathways to education, health services, housing, and means of securing a driver's license that, among other things, assist with obtaining employment.
- Increase immigrant political opportunities. The decline in violent crime is more dramatic in cities with favorable political contexts for immigrants including sanctuary cities and where limits are placed on the enforcement of immigration laws by local-level officers.

2. Immigration and the Justice System

- Protect victims of crime regardless of immigration status. One collateral consequence of heightened scrutiny of immigration status by law enforcement includes the avoidance of any and all contact with the criminal justice system including reduced cooperation and reporting of crime and victimization. Pathways to reporting violence and victimization should be barrier-free and victims and their advocates should not fear prosecution when reporting or receiving assistance.
- Terminate immigration enforcement at the local level and preserve centralized enforcement responsibilities and the basic tenets of community-oriented policing. Crime reporting and cooperation with the police is imperative for public safety for all U.S. residents. Current trends characterized by the devolution of policing responsibilities creates pressure on local law enforcement to become immigration enforcers; a strategy in stark contrast to the commitment to community-oriented policing and one that instead reduces public trust in the police, undercuts public safety, increases the risk of victimization among immigrants, and strains scarce resources among local-level law enforcement.
- Return to separate immigration and criminal courts. The fusion of immigration and criminal law is a relatively recent modification to legal code that has engendered the fusion of immigrant and criminal, and the criminalization of a group of people irrespective of behavior.
- Prioritize public safety efforts based on characteristics or severity of offenses by focusing policing strategies on targeting harmful behavior rather than certain groups of people.
- Guarantee council for immigrant defendants. Legal assistance fosters compliance and trust in the legal system. Given the strain already placed on public defender offices around the U.S., additional funding

should be allocated to support immigrants who are indigent and cannot afford an attorney.

- End the use of private prisons to detain immigrants regardless of immigrant status (e.g., asylum seeker, awaiting immigration court, or identified for removal). The use of private prisons treats immigrants as commodities for profit. Moreover, lobby banks to cut financial ties with private companies that run privately held prisons and/ or detention centers to house immigrants. There is evidence of movement in this direction as some banks have already terminated their relationship with these companies, such as Bank of America and SunTrust.

3. Immigration and Public Perceptions

- Disassociate immigration and criminality in political, public, and media discourse – language matters. The vast majority of immigrants arrive to the U.S. through legal pathways. The practice of presuming illegality is racist and produces a host of social, political, humanitarian, and criminal justice collateral damages. Productive debate cannot ensue if the public is inundated with stereotypical depictions of the immigrant-criminal. This could be done in the following ways:
  - Produce public education and language campaigns on immigration and crime to reduce inaccurate perceptions and rhetoric on the relationship between immigration and crime. This includes more traditional outlets, such as television and radio, but also more contemporary outlets such as social media (e.g., Facebook). By tapping different outlets, such campaigns will have a wider reach to diverse audiences.
  - Educate the media on the correct language to use when referencing individuals who are foreign-born to reduce the spread of inaccurate perceptions and bias-laden discourse.
  - Include migrant narratives in U.S. reporting so they have a voice in the public sphere (e.g., their lived experiences), including the effect immigration and immigration-crime policies have on them and their communities.
- Educate the public on the benefits of immigration. According to National Academy of Science reports, immigration spurs economic benefits as well as individual benefits and presents much evidence of the likely disastrous economic and fiscal costs resulting from mass deportation. Including these narratives in media reports, and other avenues that reach the wider public will provide a counterbalance

to the current media emphasis on the purported negative aspects of immigration and related enforcement campaigns.

4. Immigration and Crime Research

- Crime research (trends, disparities, offending, victimization) is significantly hindered by the lack of available and detailed data on ethnicity, immigration, and documented status. Disparities across racial and ethnic groups are biased when data are limited to a Black/White dichotomy. Data at the federal and local levels need to not only continually collect this data, but to use consistent metrics for comparative purposes.
- There should be continued research, both qualitative and quantitative, on immigration and crime, including the social, political, and criminal justice ramifications of criminalizing immigrants, using multiple sources of data (e.g., publicly available data, state- and/or federal-level data, policing data, deportation data).
- Advance new lines of research.
  - Investigate immigrant assimilation to U.S. culture in relation to subsequent increases in crime across multiple immigration generations.
  - In light of the remarkably resilient finding that foreign-born immigrants have comparatively low rates of involvement in crime, greater attention should be directed to identifying what appear to be protective factors that uniquely buffer the foreign-born from criminogenic forces. A better understanding of the buffers to offending may allow for the diffusion of these protective factors to all individuals regardless of place of birth and immigrant generation.

Key Resources

Bersani, Bianca E. 2014. "An Examination of First and Second Generation Immigrant Offending Trajectories." *Justice Quarterly* 31(2):315–343. https://doi.org/10.1080/07418825.2012.659200.

Chaves, Leo R. 2008. *The Latino Threat: Constructing Immigrants, Citizens, and the Nation.* Stanford: Stanford University Press.

Ewing, Walter A., Daniel E. Martínez, and Rubén G. Rumbaut. 2015. *The Criminalization of Immigration in the United States.* Washington, DC: American Immigration Council Special Report.

Kirk, David S., Andrew V. Papachristos, Jeffrey Fagan, and Tom R. Tyler. 2012. "The Paradox of Law Enforcement in Immigrant Communities: Does Tough Immigration Enforcement Undermine Public Safety?" *The ANNALS of the American Academy of Political and Social Science* 641:79–98. https://doi.org/10.1177/0002716211431818.

Lyons, Christopher J., María B. Vélez, and Wayne A. Santoro. 2013. "Neighborhood Immigration, Violence, and City-level Immigrant Political Opportunities." *American Sociological Review* 78(4):604–632. https://doi.org/10.1177/0003122413491964.

National Academies of Sciences, Engineering, and Medicine. 2017. *The Economic and Fiscal Consequences of Immigration.* Washington, DC: The National Academies Press. https://doi.org/10.17226/23550.

National Academies of Sciences, Engineering, and Medicine. 2015. *The Integration of Immigrants into American Society.* Washington, DC: The National Academies Press. https://doi.org/10.17226/21746.

Ousey, Graham C., and Charis E. Kubrin. 2018. "Immigration and Crime: Assessing a Contentious Issue." *Annual Review of Criminology* 1:63–84. doi: 10.1146/annurev- criminol-032317-092026.

Provine, Doris Marie, Monica W. Varsanyi, Paul G. Lewis, and Scott H. Decker. 2016. *Policing Immigrants: Local Law Enforcement on the Front Lines.* Chicago, IL: University of Chicago Press.

Stumpf, Juliet. 2006. "The Crimmigration Crisis: Immigrants, Crime, and Sovereign Power." *American University Law Review* 56:367–419.

TWELVE

Alleviating the Mark of a Criminal Record: Prison Programming and Post-Incarceration Employment

Sadé L. Lindsay

The Problem

The U.S. incarcerates 2.3 million people and 95 percent of these individuals will eventually return to their communities. Today, approximately 5 million formerly incarcerated people live in the U.S. Despite these statistics, the U.S. provides relatively few pathways for formerly incarcerated people to successfully reintegrate into society. Recidivism rates – rates of reoffending, rearrests, reconvictions, and re-incarceration – indicate just how difficult reintegration is for people returning home from prison. A 2018 Bureau of Justice Statistics report that tracked prisoners who were released in 2005 found that nearly half were rearrested during their first year of release and 80 percent were rearrested within six years of release.

Formerly incarcerated people who maintain stable, quality employment can better provide for themselves and their families and are less likely to recidivate. However, the job search process is challenging and complicated to navigate with a criminal record. A 2018 Prison Policy Initiative report estimates an unemployment rate of 27 percent among formerly incarcerated people, which is five times the national average of 5.2 percent and higher than the U.S. unemployment rate has *ever* been. High unemployment rates among formerly incarcerated people cannot be attributed to a lack of motivation to work as 93 percent of formerly incarcerated people are either employed or actively looking for work, while the same is true for 84 percent of the general public.

There are, however, two well-documented challenges formerly incarcerated people face when seeking employment. First, employers discriminate against formerly incarcerated people due to stigma surrounding their criminal histories. Second, formerly incarcerated people generally lack marketable job skills and education that would make them competitive applicants. Policymakers propose prison programming and credentialing as solutions to alleviate these causes of high unemployment rates among this population. Yet, poor access to prison programs and low levels of motivation to participate among incarcerated people most at risk limit the potential effectiveness of prison programs. In this chapter, I first identify who is largely affected by mass incarceration and reentry. Then, I highlight research and policies that address post-prison employment barriers and prison educational and training program issues. Lastly, this chapter concludes with recommendations to improve reentry efforts.

The Research Evidence

Who is Affected by Mass Incarceration and Reentry?

Challenges of mass incarceration and reentry disproportionately alter the lives of young Black and Hispanic men from impoverished communities. According to a 2017 Bureau of Justice Statistics report, Blacks make up 12 percent of the U.S. population but 33 percent of the prison population, while Whites comprise 64 percent of the U.S. population and 30 percent of prisoners. Likewise, a recent Prison Policy Initiative report finds that Hispanic adults are 3.1 times more likely to be incarcerated than White adults for the same crimes. Racial disparities are evident by the proportion of people in the U.S. who have ever been to prison or are living with felony criminal records. A 2017 study by Sarah Shannon and colleagues finds 15 percent of the entire U.S. Black adult male population had been to prison and 33 percent of the U.S. Black adult male population lives with a felony criminal record.

There are also vast educational disparities in the likelihood of imprisonment. A 2014 report by the Department of Education finds that the highest level of educational attainment for 30 percent of imprisoned people is less than a GED or high school diploma compared to only 14 percent of U.S. households. Race further compounds disparities in imprisonment by educational attainment. Becky Pettit's 2012 book estimates that Black men aged 20–34 *with* and *without* a high school diploma have a 21 percent and 68 percent chance of incarceration, respectively. The same figures for White men are 6 percent and 28 percent. Educational disparities are particularly pernicious given that jobs often require skills or at least credentials beyond a high school diploma or equivalent. Such large differences in the chance of imprisonment have implications for broader U.S. racial and economic inequality, making prisoner reentry an important contemporary, social problem.

Post-Incarceration Employment

Employment is key to the livelihoods of formerly incarcerated people and to weakening the cyclical nature of imprisonment in the U.S. Obtaining stable post-prison work provides these individuals with viable opportunities to change, demonstrate redeemable qualities, and obtain financial support. Work makes reoffending costly for formerly incarcerated people by increasing positive social ties to other people with conventional, crime-free behaviors and beliefs. But these positive effects are only likely to occur when formerly incarcerated people hold quality, stable jobs, where they feel attached to, enjoy, and/or care about the work they do.

However, formerly incarcerated people experience extreme difficulties finding stable, quality employment. Many employers ask about applicants' criminal histories during the hiring process, particularly via criminal history questions on applications. Groundbreaking research by Devah Pager (2008) suggests having a felony record reduces the chances of receiving an employer callback for an interview by 50 percent. Similar patterns persist for low-level, misdemeanor arrests and the effects are even greater for formerly incarcerated people who commit violent or sexual offenses. As a result, the stigma surrounding a criminal record often results in joblessness or reduces opportunities to low-wage, low-skilled work. This type of employment does not provide formerly incarcerated people with the means to be financially self-sufficient, nor does it result in social attachment to work and positive peers associated with reductions in reoffending.

Race and gender employment discrimination further aggravates the effects of criminal records. The Prison Policy Initiative reports that a criminal record increases unemployment rates by 37 percentage points for Black women, 28 percentage points for Black men, 18.9 percentage points for White women, and 14 percentage points for White men. These racial and gender disparities are consistent with Devah Pager's research findings that employers were *equally likely* to call White men *with felonies* for an interview as they were Black men *without felonies*.

These inequalities are especially concerning, given technological advances that make finding any run-in with the law one click away, regardless of whether these instances result in a conviction.

Research highlighting the negative effects of criminal records on employment helped government efforts to address post-incarceration employment barriers. At the federal level, the Equal Employment Opportunity Commission updated its best practice guidelines for employers using arrest and conviction records in 2012. Still, people with criminal records are not a protected class under Title VII of the Civil Rights Act, making these guidelines merely suggestive while doing little to hold employers accountable. If company policies regarding criminal records disproportionately affect a protected class under Title VII (e.g. race or gender), disparate impact discrimination lawsuits can be filed, though these are difficult to prove. A more promising approach to reducing employment challenges has been providing employers with incentives for hiring formerly incarcerated people. For example, the Work Opportunity Tax Credit gives tax credits to businesses that hire groups with traditionally high unemployment rates, including people with felony records.

State and local legislators have acted by implementing fair chance laws, such as "ban the box." These policies prohibit employers from asking criminal background questions in the initial stages of the hiring process to reduce chances of discrimination, and require employers to judge applicants solely by their qualifications. Since 1998, 35 states and over 150 cities have adopted variations of ban the box laws in private and public sector work. Unfortunately, ban the box has some unintended effects on racial discrimination in employment. A 2017 study by researchers Amanda Agan and Sonja Starr finds these policies may encourage racial discrimination. Where criminal record questions are included on applications, White applicants received 7 percent more callbacks than Black applicants. After ban the box was implemented, the Black/White gap in employer callbacks grew to 43 percent. This suggests employers in ban the box states who have limited information about criminal histories rely on an exaggerated sense of racial differences in felony criminal records and discriminate against all Black applicants, regardless of criminal histories.

Prison Educational and Job Training Programs

U.S. prisons have provided programming for incarcerated populations since the late 1800s, most of which were religious and ethics courses with specific goals of moral rehabilitation. Beginning in the 1980s when the aims of punishment shifted to focus on reducing recidivism and prison populations, more practical educational and job training programs were offered in prisons. Prison training programs have the potential to address major contributors to unemployment rates among formerly incarcerated people, making them a target of policy efforts. Prison certificates and program participation increase post-incarceration employment chances and wages, and lower prison misconduct and recidivism. Prison credentials may help close Black/White wage gaps among formerly incarcerated people. John Tyler and Jeffrey Kling's 2006 study finds no difference in the effect of a prison GED on post-release earnings among Whites but discover a 20 percent increase in earnings among nonwhites who obtained a prison GED.

Yet, demand for prison educational and job training programs far outweighs the availability of these resources. According to a 2014 Department of Education (DOE) report, incarcerated people rank vocational and educational training as the most desirable types of programs, but they often encounter long waitlists or are not selected to participate. The lack of program availability also causes incarcerated people who are required to complete certain programs as a term of their sentence to sometimes stay beyond their release dates. Moreover, there are gender differences in prison programming availability and use. Courtney Crittenden and Barbara Koons-Witt's 2017 study finds incarcerated women are more likely to have access to rehabilitative programs (e.g. substance abuse), work assignments, and educational courses, and are also more likely to participate in prison programs than incarcerated men. Insufficient programming hinders incarcerated people's ability to advance educationally and acquire requisite job skills. The DOE reports about 60 percent of adult prisoners completed no further education and only 21 percent obtained a high school diploma while incarcerated.

In addition to access, motivating at-risk incarcerated populations to participate in programs is an issue policymakers and practitioners face. Program enrollment often relies on factors such as good behavior and time to release, which means people who might benefit most from prison programs due to their higher risks of recidivism are either not selected or simply choose not to participate. The federal government has attempted to address concerns around prison program access and prisoner motivation by passing both the Second Chance Act (SCA) in 2007 and the First Step Act (FSA) in 2018. The SCA funnels federal grants to states in support of reentry-based programs, many of which focus on employment and job readiness. The FSA incentivizes program participation with good time credits that reduce prison sentences for non-violent offenders and ideally increase motivation to engage in prison programs. It also establishes a recidivism risk assessment to advise the Federal Bureau of Prisons on the types of programming each incarcerated person should participate in to lower their risk of reoffending.

State legislators have attempted to address restrictions that bar felons or people with criminal records from obtaining occupational licenses. According to a 2018 report by the Institute of Justice, 20 percent of Americans need a license to work. Trades that are widely offered in prison, such as cosmetology and barber school, require licenses to work upon release. Twenty-nine states have reformed occupational licensing laws since 2015, with hopes of easing formerly incarcerated people's ability to use skills learned in prison trade programs. These reforms vary from legislators creating new laws that completely prohibit licensure boards from denying people a license based on their criminal histories to preventing these boards from using vague language about moral character to justify license denials for people with criminal records.

Recommendations and Solutions

Even if prisons and jails were to return to pre-mass incarceration levels in the U.S., the consequences of criminal justice expansion would last for many years because of the durable criminal stigma formerly incarcerated people continue to experience. The past two decades have resulted in a substantial amount of research attention and resources allocated to address collateral consequences of imprisonment, particularly post-prison employment. Yet, there is still major work to be done. Collaborations among researchers, practitioners, (formerly) incarcerated people, and policymakers are essential, as each brings a different perspective necessary for solving prison programming and post-prison employment challenges. The following are recommendations for addressing these pressing social problems.

1. Expand Policies Incentivizing Prison Program Participation

States should follow federal policies, such as the FSA, and extend prison program participation incentives to incarcerated people in state prisons, which hold over 1.3 million people. Policies reducing sentences through good time credits for program participation can motivate incarcerated people who would not typically advance their educational training, and address low educational and skill levels to increase employability. Still, incentivizing program participation through phone privileges, preferred unit transfers, and sentence reductions may increase immediate motivations for incarcerated people to further their education but not long-term efforts that could shape reentry. These incentives should also consider ways to increase formerly incarcerated people's long-term motivations to change and further their training. Moreover, to make a meaningful impact on the broader prison population, some incentives must be granted to violent offenders, who make up most people sentenced in state prisons.

2. Increase Access to Federal and State Prison Education and Job Training Programs

Apprenticeship and trade credentialing programs are advantageous for formerly incarcerated people to signal particular skillsets to obtain jobs in their chosen field. These types of programs develop both hard skills like typing and soft skills such as communication and teamwork, which are necessary to be competitive in the labor market. In addition to increasing access to trade and job training programs, state and federal governments should restore educational resources like Pell Grants, which were largely eliminated by the Violent Crime Control and Law Enforcement Act of 1994. Unfortunately, GEDs are no longer sufficient to remain competitive and potentially counter the mark of a criminal record in the labor market.

3. Reform Occupational Licensing Restrictions and Implement Fee Reductions

Prison credentialing programs will only impact formerly incarcerated people's ability to find jobs in their fields if they are able to obtain required occupational licenses. States should continue removing policies that prevent people with criminal records from obtaining occupational licenses. Specifically, other states should follow places like Illinois and North Carolina that bar licensure boards from denying people with criminal records a license, unless the criminal record is directly related to employment duties. In addition to restrictions, occupational licensing fees are expensive, especially for formerly incarcerated people who are generally economically disadvantaged. An Institute of Justice report found occupational licensing fees were more than $260. State and federal prisons could relieve this financial burden by guaranteeing funding to obtain at least one occupational license for people who complete prison vocational programs.

4. Increase Oversight of Hiring Practices to Ensure Employers Comply with Policies Prohibiting Criminal Background-Based Discrimination

Holding companies accountable for discrimination is effective in reducing bias. State and/or local governments could implement systems for people with criminal records to report perceived employer discrimination and non-compliance, which eases the ability to investigate companies with multiple violations. States could then audit companies with repeat complaints to ensure compliance with fair chance laws and assess sanctions accordingly. Additionally, states could model an employer records system after the Housing Mortgage Disclosure Act, which requires banks to maintain records of all mortgage applications, including characteristics about applicants and reasons why applicants are denied loans. Such records could be used to further investigate claims of non-compliance with state policies that protect people with criminal records.

5. Expand Employer Incentives for Hiring People with Felony Records

The federal government could allot states funding to expand employer incentives like those in the federal Work Opportunity Tax Credit. New policies should remove limitations on when employers can use incentives to have a larger impact on reducing unemployment rates. Currently, federal tax credits only apply to those who are hired within one year of their conviction or release from prison. Additionally, to receive the business incentive, policymakers should create minimum wage requirements and stipulations on types of positions formerly incarcerated people are hired to work within companies. These conditions would prevent businesses from taking advantage of tax credits while only hiring formerly incarcerated people in low-quality, low-wage work that provides few opportunities for career advancement.

6. Increase Funding for Systematic, Longitudinal Evaluations of Prison Programs

Most evaluations measure individual program effectiveness. While this form of program evaluation is important, there should be an increased effort to fund projects or hire researchers to conduct longitudinal evaluations that compare and identify prison programs that positively affect post-prison employment chances, among other post-release outcomes. Such an effort would require both quantitative and qualitative assessments of program structure, instruction quality and effectiveness, and post-release outcomes over time. These types of evaluations would allow programs that work well to be replicated or standardized across facilities while also providing prison staff with the flexibility to modify programs to fit the needs of their prison population.

Key Resources

Bushway, Shawn D., Michael A. Stoll, and David Weiman, eds. 2007. *Barriers to Reentry? The Labor Market for Released Prisoners in Post-Industrial America.* New York: Russell Sage Foundation.

Couloute, Lucius, and Daniel Kopf. 2018. "Out of Prison & Out of Work: Unemployment among Formerly Incarcerated People." *Prison Policy Initiative Report.*

Garland, David. 2012. *The Culture of Control: Crime and Social Order in Contemporary Society.* Chicago: University of Chicago Press.

Laub, John H., and Robert J. Sampson. 2003. *Shared Beginnings, Divergent Lives: Delinquent Boys to Age 70.* Cambridge, MA: Harvard University Press.

National Research Council. 2014. *The Growth of Incarceration in the United States: Exploring Causes and Consequences.* Committee on Causes and Consequences of High Rates of Incarceration, J. Travis, B. Western, and S. Redburn, Editors. Committee on Law and Justice, Division of Behavioral and Social Sciences and Education. Washington, DC: The National Academies Press.

Pager, Devah. 2008. *Marked: Race, Crime, and Finding Work in an Era of Mass Incarceration.* Chicago: University of Chicago Press.

Pettit, Becky. 2012. *Invisible Men: Mass Incarceration and the Myth of Black Progress.* New York: Russell Sage Foundation.

Rampey, Bobby D., Shelley Keiper, Leyla Mohadjer, Tom Krenzke, Jianzhu Li, Nina Thornton, and Jacquie Hogan. 2016. *Highlights from the US PIAAC Survey of Incarcerated Adults: Their Skills, Work Experience, Education, and Training: Program for the International Assessment of Adult Competencies.* Washington, DC: U.S. Department of Education.

Vuolo, Mike, Sarah Lageson, and Christopher Uggen. 2017. "Criminal Record Questions in the Era of 'Ban the Box.'" *Criminology & Public Policy* 16(1): 139–165.

Western, Bruce. 2018. *Homeward: Life in the Year After Prison.* New York: Russell Sage Foundation.

SECTION V

Enduring Challenges

THIRTEEN

Ending the Persistence of Homelessness

R. Neil Greene and Wayne Centrone

The Problem

Homelessness has been with us for generations and the problem shows no real sign of ending. Despite rapid innovation in homelessness services and indicators of success over the last few decades, hundreds of thousands of people can still be counted on the streets and in shelters in the United States on any given night. Homelessness is also increasingly criminalized. In this chapter, we argue that despite being in an era in which we have a lot of information about homelessness, making a difference will require shifts in thinking and practice. These include broadly viewing homelessness as a social symptom that can be treated, respecting common humanity, prioritizing social equity, coordinating efforts across services and sectors, and improving prevention and coordinated response efforts. Such changes can facilitate better access to and quality within housing, employment, and health and social services. After briefly reviewing the history of homelessness in the United States and describing our current state of knowledge, we further elaborate on our recommendations.

Numerous scholars have described the history of homelessness in the United States alongside changing social factors—industrialization, the great depression, the New Deal, and nuanced contemporary times. Attention has ebbed and flowed, with varied concern and relationships between public and private sectors. The tail end of the era of deinstitutionalization—a period of time in which people were transferred out of the confined spaces of asylums and into community oriented care—is often associated with increased homelessness, but deinstitutionalization as a primary cause is disputed and, importantly, this period coincided with a confluence of additional factors such as reductions to welfare (including the dismantling of social sector housing), wage stagnation, declining union strength, growing income inequality, and rising housing costs. In any event, greater public exposure to extreme poverty and homelessness during this period precipitated a movement of sorts. Organizations such as the Community for Creative Non-Violence, led by the likes of charismatic leaders like Mitch Snyder, conducted hunger strikes, tent-city protests, and housing marches to advocate for housing as a basic human right.

The passage of the McKinney–Vento Homelessness Assistance Act of 1987 was a legislative success. McKinney–Vento funds transitional housing, job training, primary care, education, and permanent housing. Private and public sector funding converged at this time as well. Healthcare for the Homeless (HCH) programs began as demonstration projects in the early 1980s, with programs in 19 cities funded by the Robert Wood Johnson Foundation, Pew Charitable Trust, and the U.S. Conference of Mayors. Later, HCH was federally authorized under McKinney–Vento. The program is now situated under the Consolidated Health Center Program. Illustrating the influence and growth of such programs, The National Association of Community Health Centers reports that 299 health centers received federal funding under the Health Care for the Homeless program in 2017. Increased funding and infrastructure led to greater attention to inclusion and exclusion criteria for services. Defining and categorizing people experiencing homelessness has not been easy, though.

At present, The United States Department of Housing and Urban Development (HUD) defines homelessness as inclusive of the following abbreviated criteria: 1) People who are living in places not meant for human habitation; 2) People who are losing their primary nighttime residence within 14 days; 3) Unaccompanied youth; and, 4) People attempting to flee domestic violence. In comparison, The Health Resources and Services Administration (HRSA) defines homelessness as follows: Individuals who lack housing (without regard to whether the individual is a member of a family), including an individual whose primary residence during the night is a supervised public or private facility that provides temporary living accommodations and individuals who are resident in transitional housing.

Despite formal definitions, and predating them, people without permanent homes (or families to live with) have been disparagingly called "bums," "vagrants," and "hobos" over various time periods. Moreover, homelessness is perhaps most accurately described as an *experience* and one that is different for each person caught in it. This is generally broken down into three experiential groupings often used to describe subgroups: transient, episodic, and chronic. The majority of people experiencing homelessness face transient homelessness – they lose a domicile situation, find their way into unstable housing (e.g., shelters, cars, sofa surfing, or camps) and then rebuild their resources to leverage a more stable if not permanent situation.

Contemporary scholars have argued that we are now in the "new homelessness" era, one in which we know a lot about the problem and there is focus on prevention. And yet, shortages of affordable housing and emergency shelter are well documented and cities across the country continue to prohibit camping in public, sleeping in vehicles, asking for money, and food sharing. People experiencing homelessness are also targets of violence. Reports suggest that the criminalization of homelessness is increasing while more people and families are experiencing homelessness.

The Research Evidence

Point-in-time counts found that 552,830 people were experiencing homelessness on a single night in 2018. In 2019 counts found 568,000 people, an increase of roughly 3 percent. But this number is only a fraction of those experiencing homelessness over the course of a year. The National Association of Community Health Centers reported serving 1.4 million people experiencing homelessness in 2018. The most recent estimates from the National Center for Homeless Education (2017) reported 1.36 million homeless students.

Homelessness data sources include Annual Homelessness Assessment Reports (AHAR), which have been submitted to Congress since 2005 and include publicly available raw data files from the point-in-time counts. Much can also be learned from administrative datasets within homelessness services organizations. At a more aggregate level, continuum of care (CoC) integrates common data elements using electronic health records and homelessness management information systems (HMIS). Linking datasets can be particularly insightful. For example, homelessness services administrative data can be linked with mortality data from the offices of medical investigators and/or national death indices, and can be used to study trends in mortality rates and causes of death over time.

Systematic reviews on homelessness abound. A recent PubMed search for "homeless" and "systematic review" yielded 134 citations including reviews on LGBTQ+ youth homelessness, health interventions for communicable diseases, and palliative care. According to the current state of knowledge on homelessness, it is a complex and nuanced social problem with myriad macro and micro factors. It is related to poverty, racism, affordable housing, domestic violence, and access to resources and opportunity. It is also related to alcohol and drug use. People experiencing homelessness have an accelerated age-adjusted mortality rate up to 3 to 4 times that of the general population. Studies show the average age of death for a person experiencing homelessness is roughly 40–50 years. Although housing and acute care are important, researchers have found that increased and improved services provision is not necessarily related to changes in the number of people dying without a stable place to live. Rather, studies have found shifting medically determined causes of death across time. Whereas HIV/AIDS deaths were more common in the 1980s and 1990s, opioid-related deaths are more common at present. We might better understand the health needs of people experiencing homelessness by acknowledging the impact of trauma and toxic stress on the life course as well as strongly looking at fundamental causes of health disparities. We know a lot about homelessness, but have not ended it.

Recommendations and Solutions

Given the history of homelessness and its complexity, policy and social action suggestions risk pushback and failure. It should be noted that many leaders and advocacy organizations have proposed good ideas related to housing, services, income, health care, and social connectedness. This chapter builds on this foundation using a multi-disciplinary and intersectional lens. As such, the following include a blend of large-scale societal worldview changes and more concrete suggestions for policy and social action. To begin, we need leadership and a body politic that respects our common humanity and encourages a collective willingness to help our poorest neighbors. A gestalt switch is needed, from blame and anger to concern for the most vulnerable among us. This is a prerequisite for the following recommendations: 1) Recognize homelessness as a social symptom that can be treated; 2) Respect common humanity by decriminalizing homelessness; 3) Improve social equity through affordable housing and universal health care; 4) Build a safety-net across civil-sector, non-governmental, and faith-based coalitions; and 5) Improve tracking of homelessness and poverty indicators and coordinated responses.

1. Recognize Homelessness as a Social Symptom that can be Treated

We can create conditions (e.g., economic inequality and diminished support for people in need) in which the experience of homelessness is more likely. In this view, homelessness is a sign or symptom of larger social factors. Changing our social prognosis will require citizens and leaders to recognize the connection between our individual lives and experiences and structural factors. We must elect and support policymakers that seek to end conditions that increase homelessness and support collaborative efforts to end it. We must do this because the experience of homelessness is about us, as a society, not them as others within it. Solving this problem can't just be about money, although that will undoubtedly be of concern. Rather, our framing has to be about the quality of our society—and ourselves as participants within it.

2. Respect Common Humanity by Decriminalizing Homelessness

At present, the signs and symptoms of homelessness are often punished. Tent cities are broken up and removed along with personal possessions by law enforcement; panhandling and even the act of giving food or money is made illegal. Quality of life ordinances make public activity and hygiene open to police intervention. Such policies are primarily aimed at keeping homelessness out of sight—for the benefit of those who are better off—not at ending homelessness or addressing its causes. Criminalizing homelessness paints it as inherently bad and encourages othering the poorest among us. This encourages blind eyes to social problems and people in need. We must move beyond blaming individuals for problems, and toward transcending difference and seeing people as people. The National Law Center of Homelessness and Poverty is at the forefront of documenting and challenging homelessness criminalization.

3. Improve Social Equity through Affordable Housing and Universal Health Care

The historical and lifetime accumulation of advantage and disadvantage by different groups influences resources for everyone. True equity means that those who need more may receive more. Equitable approaches to housing and health care would eliminate many of the causes of homelessness and would allow people who become homeless to quickly escape those conditions.

Making housing a right would return us to the origins of the homeless and unhoused advocacy movement. Housing First models have moved us in this direction by removing barriers to housing. This momentum is helpful, but there is not enough affordable housing. Policies should aim to improve the number of affordable housing units available, ensure mixed-income housing (so as to not segregate low-income people and families), and strengthen existing fair housing and anti-discrimination policies. The National Low Income Housing Coalition is at the forefront of this work. In addition, universal health care access and coverage would ensure that people do not become homeless because of medical bills and that people do not have exacerbated health outcomes because of inability to pay for preventative care for early-stage health conditions. We should push for parity-driven health care remuneration that qualifies mental, physical, and substance use disorders and diseases in a similar way. These policies would minimize causes of homelessness, value our shared humanity, and benefit a wide range of social and economic groups.

4. Build a Safety-Net across Civil-Sector, Non-Governmental, and Faith-Based Coalitions

Policies that encourage collaboration across services and sectors are also needed. This might best be illustrated through an example that connects early interventions for mothers living in poverty. Cross-services collaboration might work to improve access to quality daycare, increase training, and pay for daycare workers who provide trauma-informed care, and include funding and resources to help families stay in housing rather than face eviction. Additional collaborative efforts might include making substance use treatment more accessible while recognizing the role of peer providers in preventing relapse. Alongside these efforts, we could advocate vocational training programs that incorporate life skills enhancement and coaching services after entering a new job. We can begin collaborative work like this by supporting a more integrated model of services delivery.

5. Improve Tracking of Homelessness and Poverty Indicators and Coordinated Responses

We currently rely on once a year point-in-time counts for annual homelessness assessments, but conditions can change quickly and much can be missed in between counting efforts. Pairing these counts with additional metrics and indicators can help. Many cities and communities are conducting death reviews and have created systems that involve public health, hospitals, service organizations, and other advocacy groups in the process of assessing numbers, causes, and locations of deaths of people without homes in their jurisdictions. Homeless death review teams have been formalized in Philadelphia,

New York, Sacramento, and San Francisco among other cities and more cities are developing such teams. Annual death counts show steady numbers of people dying without a place to live and many are not involved with local homelessness services. Tracking deaths raises attention to the most severe health outcome and can precipitate quicker community action. This work requires coordination between organizations, facilitates the sharing of best practices, and can help improve access to and quality of services. Further, such work has moved communities toward inclusive and standardized definitions of homelessness, and strengthened arguments for affordable housing and housing-first programing. Tracking housing status as a "vital sign" is another key opportunity. Linking health status and housing status would allow providers to identify at-risk or vulnerable populations and focus services delivery.

In summary, there is a long history of homelessness in the United States and a strong body of research about it. Despite knowing a lot about homelessness, we have not ended it. Resistance to change among the machineries of the status quo has always been strong, but reshaping the social world is possible. We must view homelessness as a societal problem—that can be treated—and we must work together, across formal and informal groups and organizations. We can move in this direction by advocating recovery, being inclusive, and fostering belonging. We must come to see that caring for the poorest and most vulnerable among us is good and is something that everyone can do. Homelessness has persisted for generations, but it is a problem that can be solved. Our worldview matters.

Key Resources

Baggett, Travis. P., Stephen W. Hwang., James J. O'Connell, Bianca C. Porneala, Erin J. Stringfellow, E. John Oray, Daniel E. Singer, Nancy A. Rigotti. 2013. "Mortality among Homeless Adults in Boston: Shifts in Causes of Death over a 15-Year Period." *JAMA Internal Medicine* 173:189–195. DOI: 10.1001/jamainternmed.2013.1604

Cronley, Courtney. 2010. "Unraveling the Social Construction of Homelessness." *Journal of Human Behavior in the Social Environment* 20:313–333. DOI: 10.1080/10911350903269955

Fowler, Patrick J., Peter S. Hovmand, Katherine E. Marcal, and Sanmay Das. 2019. "Solving Homelessness from a Complex Systems Perspective: Insights for Prevention Responses." *Annual Review of Public Health* 465. DOI: 10.1146/annurev-publhealth-040617-013553

Institute of Medicine Committee on Health Care for Homeless People. 1988. *Dynamics of Homelessness. Homelessness, 2. Health, and Human Needs.* Washington, DC: National Academies Press. Retrieved from: https://www.ncbi.nlm.nih.gov/books/NBK218240/

Johnson, Robert Ann. 2010. "African Americans and Homelessness: Moving Through History." *Journal of Black Studies* 40(4): 583. DOI: 10.1177/0021934708315487

Lamb, H.R. 1984. "Deinstitutionalization and the Homeless Mentally Ill." *Hospital and Community Psychiatry* 35:899–907. DOI: 10.1176/ps.35.9.899

Lee, Barrett A., Kimberly A. Tyler, and James D. Wright. 2010. "The New Homelessness Revisited." *Annual Review of Sociology* 36:501–521. DOI: 10.1146/annurev-soc-070308-115940

Mechanic, David and David A. Rochefort. 1990. "Deinstitutionalization: An Appraisal of Reform." *Annual Review of Sociology* 16:301–327. DOI: 10.1146/annurev.so.16.080190.001505

Montgomery, Ann Elizabeth, Stephen Metraux, and Dennis Culhane. 2013. "Rethinking Homelessness Prevention among Persons with Serious Mental Illness." *Social Issues and Policy Review* 7(1):58–82. DOI: 10.1177/0022146510383498

Phelan, Jo, Bruce Link, and Parisa Tehranifar. 2010. "Social Conditions as Fundamental Causes of Health Inequalities: Theory, Evidence, and Policy Implications." *Journal of Health and Social Behavior* 51:S28–S40. DOI: 10.1177/0022146510383498

Roncarati, Jill S., Travis P. Baggett, James J. O'Connell, Stephen W. Hwang, E. Francis Cook, Nancy Krieger, and Glorian Sorensen. 2019. "Mortality Among Unsheltered Homeless Adults in Boston, Massachusetts, 2000–2009." *JAMA Internal Medicine* 178(9):1242–1248. DOI: 10.1001/jamainternmed.2018.2924

Rossi, Peter H. 1989. *Down and Out in America: The Origins of Homelessness.* Chicago, IL: University of Chicago Press.

Shlay, Anne B., and Peter H. Rossi. 1992. "Social Science Research and Contemporary Studies of Homelessness." *Annual Review of Sociology* 129–160. DOI: 10.1146/annurev.so.18.080192.001021

Snow, David A., and Leon Anderson. 1993. *Down on Their Luck: A Study of Homeless Street People.* Berkeley, CA: University of California Press.

FOURTEEN

Risks to Journalists' Safety and the Vulnerability of Media Freedom in the U.S.

Sadia Jamil and Glenn W. Muschert

The Problem

Media freedom is primarily the freedom of diverse forms of media and sources of communication. Traditionally, freedom of the press is conceptualized as the freedom to publish; however, the notion of media freedom is much broader as it encompasses the freedom both to publish and to broadcast, emphasizing the idea that media in information societies consist of more than print sources (e.g. newspapers and magazines) and incorporates electronic sources of communication as well, such as radio, television, and the Internet. Hence, freedom of the media is indispensable for democratic societies given that the media are an outlet for public discussion and opinion and basically operate to seek the truth, educate the public, and serve as a watchdog over government.

Threats to journalists and attacks on media freedom undermine the proper functioning of the United States as a democratic society, as the ability of journalists to investigate and report on controversial topics becomes threatened by the government and pressure groups such as criminal gangs, terrorists, and corporate giants. In the U.S., as elsewhere, freedom of expression is a fundamental human right, and a precondition for many other democratic rights. According to the First Amendment of the U.S. Constitution:

> Congress shall make no law respecting an establishment of religion, or prohibiting the free exercise thereof; or abridging the freedom of speech, or of the press; or the right of the people peaceably to assemble, and to petition the government for a redress of grievances.

Restrictions on freedom of expression can be direct (such as stringent laws) and indirect (such as censorship pressure from the government and military), and vary relative to social contexts. In democratic systems, media organizations and journalists have been the lifeline of freedom of expression and public accountability. The existence of free and pluralistic media is indispensable to democratic governance, and media freedom is vital to the practice of journalism. Media professionals and journalists need the freedom to perform their jobs without undue constraints. Journalists report on issues of public interest, including government policies, and have a key role to play in democracies by revealing truth and disseminating information indispensable to sustainable knowledge societies. Threats and violence against journalists and media professionals can stop the public from exercising their fundamental right to seek, receive, and impart information.

As a profession, journalism attracts hostility for reporting on controversial issues such as protests and social movements, political scandals, corruption, corporate malfeasance, and organized crime. Therefore, the right of journalists to undertake their jobs under safe conditions, without fear of being harassed or attacked, is of paramount importance for media freedom and freedom of expression.

The U.S. media regularly report on the how the U.S. government's surveillance of journalists' activities is affecting their right to freedom of expression. Although the U.S. has historically been seen as a leading example of a nation which values press freedom and protects journalists, it now seems that this is no longer so, as the safety of journalists and the preservation of press freedom are being eroded. In previous decades, the U.S. ranked very highly worldwide for such factors as democratic vigour, public welfare, freedom of expression and information, and absence of corruption. Thus it is particularly troubling that U.S. journalists' voices (both offline and online) are increasingly silenced through threats and pressure.

International organizations monitoring the freedom of expression and safety of journalists, such as Reporters Without Borders (RSF) and the Committee to Protect Journalists, have now classified the U.S. as one of the "problematic places" for working journalists, given the increased frequency of threats to journalists. The U.S. Press Freedom Tracker's latest statistics indicate that, as of January 2020, five journalists have been attacked and one journalist has been imprisoned in the United States.

One obvious implication of the growing risks to U.S. journalists is the country's dropped ranking in the RSF Press Freedom Index 2019, in which the U.S. now ranks behind countries such as Romania,

Chile, and Botswana. However, it is not only journalists and media organizations which are at risk, but rather the role that open reporting on issues of public concern plays in the proper functioning of a knowledge society with a democratic system of governance.

The Research Evidence

Press freedom in the U.S. has declined in recent years, and there has been an increase in hostility, threats, and attacks on journalists and other media personnel. The challenge of studying such risks, however, is due to the fact there has been little research about threats to media in the U.S., as globally the country had been seen as a model case for the safety of journalists and as a guarantor of freedom of expression not only within its own borders, but also worldwide. The RSF Press Freedom Index (2019) indicates that the U.S. press freedom ranking is 48 among 180 countries evaluated.

A prominent event contributing to the decline in press freedom in the U.S. was the June 2018 mass shooting of four U.S. journalists and one sales staff member from the *Capital Gazette*, a daily newspaper in Annapolis, Maryland. The attack was supposedly motivated by retribution for the newspaper's coverage of a criminal harassment case. Such an attack on journalists is rather unprecedented in the U.S., and is an alarming sign for a country whose democratic system depends on media freedoms.

Of course, a single attack is insufficient to constitute a crisis; however, data also reveal a broader pattern of harassment and violence against U.S. journalists, which does warrant serious concern. Indeed, journalists in the U.S. are subject to physical risks, and also other types of risk that may hinder the exercise of their right to freedom of expression such as psychological, digital, gender-specific, public, and financial risks. Many U.S. journalists work within an environment of regular online harassment and attacks or abuse while on duty, and are at psychological risk including from excessive stress, trauma, anxiety, nervousness, and fear either after physical or online attacks, such as hacking, phishing, trolling, and harassment. For example, a very recent study conducted by Idas, Backholm and Korhonen (2019) suggests:

> Journalists cover potentially traumatic major events (e.g. earthquakes or terror) or smaller incidents (e.g. car accidents or criminal cases) in their line of work. Witnessing such events may result in long-term impairment such as PTSD,

characterised by symptoms such as intrusive memories, negative mood changes and avoidance of trauma reminders.

Reporters Without Borders' report (2019) suggests that U.S. journalists have become more vulnerable in their daily routines, at home, in the newsroom, and on the road. Especially as digital risks and surveillance increase, journalists may be digitally monitored and/or attacked by government entities, intelligence agencies, corporations, criminal organizations, and terrorists. Gender-based risks to journalists are widespread worldwide, and the U.S. is no exception, as women journalists are disproportionately confronted by threats of sexual abuse and online harassment.

The dilemma of U.S. journalists is not just limited to the diverse nature and sources of risks, but it is also clearly linked to the government's stance on the protection of journalists and media freedoms. Freedom House's report (2019), "Media Freedom: A Downward Spiral," suggests that the U.S. government has not been consistently supportive and proactive enough to guarantee the safety of journalists and press freedom, and this deficiency has been noted even at the highest levels. This situation is a noted shift as in previous decades, the U.S. government was a worldwide example of a system working for the protection and rights of journalists. One prominent example is the case of the *Wall Street Journal* correspondent Daniel Pearl, who was abducted and later killed in 2002 in Karachi, the southern port city of Pakistan. At that time, the U.S. government under President G. W. Bush, had called for Pakistani authorities to take immediate legal action against the British national Omar Sheikh, a main figure in the murder. In 2006, the Bush administration similarly called for the Russian government to prosecute the murder of the Russian investigative journalist Anna Politkovskaya.

Since the time when the U.S. was a global example for media freedoms, and which indeed extended its influence beyond its borders, the government's stance towards journalists has changed, which diminishes U.S. influence abroad and undermines press freedoms domestically. A 2019 report by Freedom House states:

> The most concerning development of recent years, press freedom has come under unusual pressure in the United States, the world's leading democratic power. Although key news organizations remain strong and continue to produce vigorous reporting on those in office, President Donald

Trump's continual vilification of the press has seriously exacerbated an ongoing erosion of public confidence in the mainstream media. Among other steps, the president has repeatedly threatened to strengthen libel laws, revoke the licenses of certain broadcasters, and damage media owners. other business interests. The US constitution [*sic*] provides robust protections against such actions, but President Trump's public stance on press freedom has had a tangible impact on the global landscape. Journalists around the world now have less reason to believe that Washington will come to their aid if their basic rights are violated (pp 3–4).

Thus, the stance of the U.S. President toward journalists is not only a threat to media personnel within U.S. news agencies, but it is also shaking up the democratic structure of a country that may lose its integrity in the erosion of rights to freedom of expression and the protection of journalists. In the light of foregoing facts, it is imperative to devise strategies that can help U.S. journalists to work safely and to maintain and practice freedom of expression effectively.

Recommendations and Solutions

A lack of freedom of expression and risks to journalists' safety are two different issues, but they are interrelated because journalists need to be safe personally and professionally to exercise freedom of expression in their professional and personal lives. The issue of safety of journalists in the U.S. calls for a plan of action that requires multiple strategies.

Steps towards Improving the Mental Well-Being of U.S. Journalists

U.S. journalists frequently report on natural disasters, risky criminal cases, war, and other forms of conflict. Nevertheless, dealing with the repercussion – journalists' individual emotional response – can be a challenge. Moreover, journalists often suffer from workplace stress, because of organizational pressures, and thus it is essential that they exercise self-care and are aware of their personal risks. Such resources can be provided by media organizations, but also are needed as part of professional training for media personnel. In addition, such topics should be emphasized in post-secondary journalism programs, which prepare the majority of professionals to work as journalists.

Use Digital Safety Protocols and Digital Security Training

Advancements in digital technology increase the status of journalism as a dangerous profession, but the effective use of digital safety protocols and training of journalists can mitigate these risks. The widespread use of mobile devices among journalists has been accompanied by a stream of applications that apply security layers, but before media support organizations can help make those tools available, they must first establish a baseline of the current digital practices among journalists. The following are recommendations for the digital safety of journalists:

- Journalists must become skilled in the use of digital security tools. The government's surveillance has made U.S. journalists more concerned about digital safety and more aware about their online surveillance by public and private entities. A best practice involves journalists developing proficiency in the use of digital safety tools. Such trainings can take place both within journalism programs and within media agencies.
- Journalists need to employ tools for tracking their own whereabouts and to report back to entities monitoring their safety. Reporters can be physically abused, end up in a hospital, get lost in an unfamiliar city or territory, or be abducted by hostile groups. Mobile applications are needed which permit journalists to be tracked through GPS while doing duty in a risky place. The tracking applications can help journalists to maintain a record of their movements and locations, which in turn can help editors and their colleagues to keep in touch with them.
- Journalists must become proficient in encryption of data and communications content. Journalists must encrypt data stored in electronic devices, particularly mobile devices, to prevent the theft or misuse of sensitive data. One important preventive measure can be to have encrypted files stored in the cloud so journalists do not have to store it in a hard drive, ensuring more safety of their data. Alternatively, journalists can encrypt their hard drives or files so that important information cannot be accessed if they lose their devices. They are also recommended to exercise caution while carrying their devices. This shall reduce the chances of device snatching and theft.

Academic Initiatives

Academicians in journalism schools and social science and technical disciplines more broadly should engage in continued research into media freedom and safety issues of U.S. journalists. Such academic investigation can contribute to the empowerment of journalists through enhancing their safety and press freedom rights, which ultimately allows journalists to function freely to support the robust public discourse in the democratic system. Academics need to integrate research networks into professional networks, to enhance the application of research knowledge to the practical needs of practicing journalists. Topics ripe for investigation in the U.S. include the following:

- Government's attitude towards the protection of journalists and free speech rights, and its effect on journalism practice.
- The nature and sources of threats to journalists' safety, and methods to mitigate such risks.
- Investigation of legal frameworks to ensure journalists' offline and online safety to enhance physical, psychological, digital and financial protection of journalists.
- Investigation into corporate actions and public regulatory frameworks affecting journalists and journalism.
- Investigation into the financial risks to journalists and media organizations.
- Investigation into the digitization of journalism and its associated risks, including surveillance, location monitoring, risks to journalists and their sources, and privacy issues.
- The role of media organizations and journalist unions in protecting journalists from risks.
- Development of training programs and university-level courses to inform journalists and other media professionals of the nature and types of safety risks, and measures to reduce these risks.

Key Resources

Carlsson, U., & Pöyhtäri, R. 2017. *The Assault on Journalism: Building Knowledge to Protect Freedom of Expression*. Goteborg: NORDICOM.

Committee to Protect Journalists. 2020. "1365 Journalists Killed between 1992 and 2020." Retrieved at: https://cpj.org/data/killed/?status=Killed&motiveConfirmed%5B%5D=Confirmed&type%5B%5D=Journalist&start_year=1992&end_year=2020&group_by=year

Committee to Protect Journalists. 2020. "CPJ Report: 11 Journalists Killed in the US." Retrieved from: https://cpj.org/data/killed/americas/usa/?status=Killed&motiveConfirmed%5B%5D=Confirmed&type%5B%5D=Journalist&cc_fips%5B%5D=US&start_year=1992&end_year=2020&group_by=location

Farley, R. 2019. "Another Dubious Trump Attack on 'Fake News'." Retrieved from: https://www.factcheck.org/2019/12/another-dubious-trump-attack-on-fake-news/

Freedom House. 2019. "Media Freedom 2019: A Downward Spiral." Retrieved from: https://freedomhouse.org/report/freedom-and-media/2019/media-freedom-downward-spiral

Idas, T., Backholm, K., & Korhonen, J. 2019. "Trauma in the Newsroom: Social Support, Post-Traumatic Stress and Post-Traumatic Growth among Journalists Working with Terror." *European Journal of Psychotraumatology* 10(1). https://dx.doi.org/10.1080%2F20008198.2019.1620085

Ingber, S. 2019. "The U.S. Now Ranks as A 'Problematic' Place for Journalists." Retrieved from: https://www.npr.org/2019/04/18/714625907/the-u-s-now-ranks-as-a-problematic-place-for-journalists

Jamil, S. 2020. *The Handbook of Research on Combating Threats to Media Freedom and Journalists' Safety*. Pennsylvania: IGI Global.

Reporters Without Borders. 2019. "World Press Freedom Index." Retrieved from: https://rsf.org/en/ranking

U.S. Press Freedom Tracker. 2020. "Statistics." Retrieved from: https://pressfreedomtracker.us/

FIFTEEN

Environmental Justice

David N. Pellow

The Problem

Environmental injustice (or environmental inequality) is widespread in the U.S. and around the globe. Environmental injustice is the term scholars use to describe what occurs when marginal populations suffer a disproportionately high burden of environmental harm and are excluded from environmental decisions affecting their communities. This is a social problem that primarily affects people of color, Indigenous peoples, low-income populations, immigrants, and women. These communities are sites where hazardous facilities, landfills, incinerators, toxic waste sites, and contaminated water, air, land, and food are frequently the order of the day. *Environmental racism* is a specific form of environmental inequality that impacts people of color. Many people tend to think of racism in limited terms—as language and behavior perpetrated by individual bigots. However, sociologists have determined that racism is also perpetrated on a massive scale by institutions, corporations, and governments every day. Racism is also far more than merely prejudice and discrimination, which means that in addition to causing anxiety, fear, and anger among those who suffer under its heels, it is also responsible for increased vulnerability to increased illness, disease, and death. Environmental racism is a particular form of racism and must be confronted by people, organizations, and institutions at all scales if we are to reduce its impacts in society. This chapter explores the research evidence concerning environmental injustice and racism and considers several approaches that scholars, activists, and governments have taken to address this critical social problem.

The Research Evidence

Research on environmental inequalities dates back to the early 1970s and has produced thousands of studies revealing empirical evidence of the strong spatial correlation between various social categories (e.g., race, class, immigration status) and exposure or spatial proximity to environmental pollutants. The field of scholarly research on this topic is commonly known as environmental justice studies. That field also explores and analyzes political responses to environmental inequalities, what is commonly known as the environmental justice movement.

The empirical evidence is clear that at the city, county, regional, national, and transnational scales, environmental threats hit low-income, people of color, immigrant, and Indigenous communities hardest. This includes exposure to a range of pollutants but also the impacts of climate change. There are many reasons for these disproportionate exposures, including the racial and class biases that are built into market economies, as well as the discriminatory use of policy tools such as zoning laws and practices.

One example of environmental injustice is the way human-caused climate change affects communities, nations, and regions of the globe very differently—hence the use of the term *climate injustice*. For example, climate change impacts Indigenous peoples first and foremost because coal, gas, and oil extraction industries frequently operate on the lands and waters of Indigenous peoples in ways that violate treaties that governments have signed with those communities. These treaties often guarantee the protection of these ecosystems and the flora and fauna within them by promising Indigenous people primary access to and control over those entities—a core component of Indigenous sovereignty. However, the extractive activities of many governments and corporations engaging in fossil fuel development routinely pollute the territories and bodies of Indigenous communities, thus violating their right to a clean environment (e.g., air, land, and water), health and wellbeing, and their right to say no to such projects. This is an example of environmental and climate injustice because 1) Indigenous communities are far less responsible for climate disruption because they tend to have far lower per capita energy consumption and lower levels of greenhouse gas generation than wealthier societies like the U.S., Europe, and Russia and 2) Indigenous societies are paying a higher social, economic, and ecological price for global climate disruption. The movement for environmental and climate justice worked to address climate disruption while seeking to dissolve and alleviate the unequal burdens created by that phenomenon.

Flint, Michigan has a population with a high percentage of working-class and low-income residents, and a majority of African Americans. That city recently experienced a lead poisoning crisis when an unelected official switched the primary water source for the community from the Detroit River to the Flint River. This was deeply unfortunate because the Flint River is contaminated and when the water interacted with the pipes in the city system and in people's homes, the pipes leached lead. Lead exposure in children can lead to declines in cognitive development, dramatic changes in behavior, and neurological disorders. This was a case of environmental injustice and racism because the majority of people affected were low-income and/ or African Americans.

Recommendations and Solutions

There are numerous ways to address environmental injustice, and in this section I consider three. However, before I do that, I want to underscore the importance of understanding the *depths* of the problem. Only then can we propose and enact solutions that have clear potential for success. Toward that end I would like to expand on the earlier section on "Problems" to consider what the key indicators and driving forces behind environmental injustice are. First, the major indicators of environmental injustice in marginalized communities include:

- Unequal protection and regulatory enforcement against hazardous facility placement in neighborhoods and near schools and hospitals;
- Highly polluted air, land, water, and food;
- Disproportionate occupational safety and health hazards;
- Disproportionate health problems among marginalized communities;
- Extraction of fossil fuels and other forms of ecological wealth, particularly on Indigenous lands;
- Unsafe housing;
- Uneven access to healthy, nutritious, affordable and culturally appropriate foods (also known as food injustice);
- Uneven impacts of human-caused climate disruption (also known as climate injustice).

These indicators of environmental injustice indicate formidable challenges for our societies, when people are assaulted with environmental hazards from birth to death, in their homes and neighborhoods, in spaces where people might normally assume they are safe from harm. In order to effectively address these problems, we must consider what the underlying conditions are that produce these social imbalances and harms. According to the most widely respected research on this topic, the *driving forces* of environmental injustice include:

- States and industry following the "path of least resistance" with respect to placement of polluting facilities (institutional racism and class inequalities);
- Racially and economically discriminatory housing markets;
- Exclusion from law and policy-making;
- Discriminatory zoning and planning in urban areas;
- Poverty and glaring income and wealth inequalities;
- Settler colonialism (the European invasion of Indigenous lands, resulting in the impoverishment and destruction of both peoples and ecosystems);
- Capitalism (specifically, the ways in which market economies thrive on widening social inequalities and anti-ecological practices);
- The absence of democracy and the presence of authoritarian governments.

If environmental injustice and racism are the problems we are facing, then one solution that scholars and activists have proposed is *environmental justice*. The United States Environmental Protection Agency (USEPA) defines environmental justice as the fair treatment and meaningful involvement of all people regardless of race, color, national origin, or income with respect to the development, implementation, and enforcement of environmental laws, regulations, and policies. While this definition is a good start, it is a rather narrow way of defining environmental justice. A broader approach might explain environmental justice as a goal and a vision in which no community is unfairly burdened with pollution or other environmental harms and where social justice and ecological sustainability prevail.

The foundational idea in this discussion is *justice*. Justice is a core principle of democracy and is tightly linked with environmental and climate protection. How so? Because those communities, states, and nations with stronger protections for women and other marginalized communities also tend to have stronger environmental protections. In other words, those societies with healthier indicators of social equality, democracy, and justice tend to also have stronger environmental protections as well. So if we desire ecological sustainability and climate protection, we must work to strengthen our democracies and promote social equity, and that means strengthening our social systems, which facilitate justice for all. Next, I offer three modest policy proposals for addressing environmental justice concerns.

Proposal #1: Strengthen the USEPA

Sociologist Jill Lindsey Harrison's book *From the Inside Out: The Fight for Environmental Justice within Government Agencies* explores the factors that shape how and why the United States Environmental Protection Agency so frequently fails to protect the environment and uphold the principles and policy imperatives of environmental justice. More broadly, Harrison's study is about exploring why government allows environmental inequalities to persist and go largely unchallenged. This is a seemingly simple question but it has not yet been asked by scholars from this particular vantage point. This is a disturbing and groundbreaking exploration of internal factors inside the USEPA that reveal how staff members variously promote and push back against environmental justice imperatives, underscoring a lack of unity, inconsistencies in mission definition, and deeply consequential divisions that harm both the agency's staff and communities enduring pollution. Staff members tasked with promoting environmental justice at the USEPA are small in number and lack the power to push their agenda through the agency's hierarchy, so they must work to persuade colleagues and superiors up the chain of command to take environmental justice more seriously than they otherwise would, and to see it as a core part of the agency's mission. The organizational inertia that results from this tension is a major finding that adds a long-overlooked element in the literature, which has thus far focused almost entirely on the role of conservative political elites and industry lobbyists in creating what one might call an "unpolitics of environmental justice"—the goal of watering down, minimizing, or even taking environmental justice off the regulatory table entirely. Instead, what Harrison finds is that while environmental justice staffers generally embrace and promote environmental justice (which is, after all, their job), it is their own co-workers and other staffers at the agency who provide the front lines of that inertia, that resistance, that institutional refusal, which ultimately contribute to the perpetuation of environmental racism and injustice.

Consider the following fact: in its nearly 30-year history of processing environmental discrimination complaints, the USEPA's Office of Civil Rights has reviewed nearly 300 complaints filed by communities of color living in the shadows of polluting industry, but has never once made a formal finding of a civil-rights violation. This is despite the reality that residents in literally scores of communities across the United States are forced to breath polluted air, drink polluted water, and live atop polluted land because they exist in the shadow of toxic industries that have been given a license to produce, store, and dump harmful substances regardless of the dangers and risks this entails. This harsh reality raises serious questions about how much ordinary people should be placing their faith and trust in the USEPA in particular and in the government more generally. The mostly African American residents of the University Place subdivision in Baton Rouge, Louisiana know this story all too well. They live in close proximity to a sewage treatment plant, which attracts flies and produces stomach-turning odors and air pollution each day. In 2009, residents asked the USEPA's Office of Civil Rights to investigate. That office has a single purpose—to ensure that government agencies that receive EPA funding don't engage in discrimination. That mandate stems from the federal Civil Rights Act of 1964, whose Title VI prohibits racial discrimination by institutions receiving federal financial assistance. The city of Baton Rouge is one such agency. Within months of receiving the residents' claim, the Office of Civil Rights rejected it. I note that even though the Donald J. Trump regime has done more to weaken environmental justice policies than any prior administration, the USEPA's failures span decades and include leadership under both Republican and Democratic presidencies.

Given the volumes of evidence that the USEPA is negligent and consistently enables environmental injustice and racism, we need elected officials who are willing to strengthen the agency and to insist that it carry out its mandate of non-discrimination in the service of environmental justice and protection.

Proposal #2: Revise the Commerce Clause

The Commerce Clause in the U.S. Constitution empowers the federal government to regulate domestic and international trade. That sounds like a good thing, but many proponents of hazardous waste management facilities have used that clause to maintain and strengthen their ability to import and export trash and other waste across state lines into communities fighting against environmental injustice. When environmental justice advocates and allies argue that their city or state shouldn't have to host waste produced in and exported from another state, industry advocates have often claimed that preventing such practices would violate the Commerce Clause because only the federal government has the power to regulate trade, not local communities. Waste industry supporters have won a number of environmental justice cases on the grounds that to stop or prevent such waste importation would threaten a core function of the U.S. economy.

In other words, environmental racism and the dumping of waste across state borders have been deemed a national necessity. In effect, the courts have told communities of color that dumping on them—that poisoning them with other people's waste—is in the national interest.

It is outrageous that the environmental justice movement's most basic demands—to be able to live in a community free of hazardous waste—could be declared "unconstitutional." Therefore, my proposal is that we urge elected officials and community leaders to address this problem either by revising the Commerce Clause itself or by creating a new constitutional amendment. The government must embrace environmental justice at all levels because it is a basic human right.

Proposal #3: Make No Demands on the Government, Instead Build Power

There are scholars who have taken a hard look at the empirical evidence and trends concerning environmental injustice and have concluded that there is little hope of achieving meaningful change through governmental channels. They ask "why would we expect the very institutions that have caused the problem to adopt an about-face and suddenly decide to solve the problem?" Moreover, they ask "why would ordinary people want to reinforce the kind of power that governments enjoy in hopes that they might put that power to good use when they so rarely do so?" I believe these are legitimate and fair questions, and they stem from a long history of research and activism that suggests that governments tend to be deeply hierarchical, inherently anti-ecological, and always rely on the power of force, coercion, and violence to achieve their ends. In other words, if we buy this line of reasoning, governments—and nation-states in particular—are the antithesis of the kinds of mechanisms we need to mobilize around to achieve environmental justice. If that is the case, then what are our options? It turns out, alternatives exist all around us if we only pay attention. Consider the social movements around the world that have achieved great gains for social and environmental justice without relying on formal governments and who operate instead through the use of assemblies and consensus-based decision making and the mobilization of resources from everyday people and organizations: the Zapatistas in Mexico, the global network of activist farmers known as La Via Campesina, the World Social Forum, and countless communities in rural India, Brazil, London, New York, and elsewhere. Rather than demanding rights and new laws from governments, these groups actually make change happen directly through grassroots democratic practices that have achieved major successes, including the reduction of health and economic disparities, equalizing workloads, improving ecological health, growing healthy food, and addressing the problems of homelessness and landlessness.

Taken as a whole, the three proposals speak to the question: what might environmental justice look like? While environmental justice problems and solutions vary from location to location, the evidence suggests that enduring environmental justice solutions tend to focus on the root social, ecological, political, and economic causes of our environmental and climate crises, and are more impactful and enduring if they address the need for systemic change (in other words, seeking solutions through practices and institutions that produced the problem in the first place make little sense). The evidence also indicates that community action at the local level (with allies from far and wide) can often be quite effective at building political power (whether through or outside of formal government institutions), preventing environmentally destructive policies and practices, and promoting sustainability and social equity.

Finally, I think it is imperative to emphasize why environmental justice is of such importance. Many people think of environmental justice in the same way they think of the importance of diversity: as an afterthought, as a box to be checked after the more important goals are attended to. But environmental justice is not just a box to be checked because the empirical research demonstrates that social inequality is the single most important driving force behind our ecological crises. Consider this: the first financial supports that made possible the economic system that produced global climate disruption (i.e., the industrial revolution) came from the exploitation of working class people, colonialism, conquest, genocide, and enslavement. In other words, if our global economy—the same economy that is placing global ecosystems and human life at great risk—is rooted in histories and ongoing practices of violent subjugation and brutality, then justice, equity, and diversity have to be at the center of any solutions to this challenge. The scholarship on this topic reveals clearly that social equality and democracy are beneficial to local and global ecosystems, so we now realize how intertwined human and non-human systems are and how important it is to maintain the health of both because they are inseparable.

Key Resources

Campbell, Carla, Rachael Greenberg, Deepa Mankikar, and Ronald D. Ross. 2016. "A Case Study of Environmental Injustice: The Failure in Flint." *International Journal of Environmental Research and Public Health* 13(10): 951–962.

Harrison, Jill Lindsey. 2019. *From the Inside Out: The Fight for Environmental Justice within Government Agencies*. Cambridge, MA: The MIT Press.

Lombardi, Kristen, Talia Buford, and Ronnie Greene. 2015. *Environmental Justice, Denied*. Center for Public Integrity. https://publicintegrity.org/environment/environmental-racism-persists-and-the-epa-is-one-reason-why/

Norgaard, Kari. 2019. *Salmon and Acorns Feed Our People: Colonialism, Nature, and Social Action*. New Brunswick, NJ: Rutgers University Press.

Parker, Joe. 2019. *Democracy Beyond the Nation State: Practicing Equality*. New York: Routledge.

Pellow, David N. 2017. *What is Critical Environmental Justice?* Cambridge: Polity Press.

Polletta, Francesca. 2002. *Freedom is an Endless Meeting: Democracy in American Social Movements*. Chicago: The University of Chicago Press.

Scott, James. 2009. *The Art of Not Being Governed: An Anarchist History of Upland Southeast Asia*. New Haven, CT: Yale University Press.

Taylor, Dorceta. 2014. *Toxic Communities: Environmental Racism, Industrial Pollution, and Residential Mobility*. New York: New York University Press.

Waziyatawin. 2008. *What Does Justice Look Like? The Struggle for Liberation in Dakota Homeland*. St. Paul, MN: Living Justice Press.

SIXTEEN

Protecting and Rewarding Workers in the 21st Century

Arne L. Kalleberg

The Problem

The deterioration of job quality in the United States in the past three decades has made this topic a major concern and serious challenge. The consequences of bad jobs are widespread, affecting not only experiences related to work but also many non-work individual (e.g., mental stress, poor physical health, uncertainty about educational choices), family (e.g., delayed entry into marriage and having children), and broader social (e.g., community disintegration and disinvestment) outcomes.

This worsening of the quality of jobs is reflected in two major ways. First, there is a crisis of low-wage work in the United States: Wages have stagnated for most workers and become more unequal between the top 10 percent of incomes and the bottom 90 percent (and more dramatically, between the top 1 percent and the bottom 50 percent). There has also been a rise of low-wage and very low-wage jobs, especially for workers without a college degree.

Second, there has been a rise in what has come to be known as *precarious work*, or work that is *uncertain, unstable*, and *insecure*, in which people receive *limited social benefits and statutory entitlements*, and in which the *risks of work are transferred away from employers and the government, toward workers*. These changes pose new risks for people, such as job insecurity (with respect to both losing one's job and being able to find a new one) and economic insecurity. These risks of low-wage work and insecure jobs are unevenly distributed among the labor force, as they differ according to individuals' resources and labor market power, produced both by their human capital characteristics and by their gender, race or ethnicity, age, and immigration status among other factors.

These declines in job quality are not merely outcomes of business cycles but represent major transitions that are associated with social, political, and economic forces that have radically transformed the nature of work and employment relations. Globalization has increased the amount of competition faced by companies, provided greater opportunities for them to outsource work to lower-wage countries, and opened up new sources of vulnerable workers through immigration. More knowledge-intensive work has been accompanied by an accelerated pace of innovation in information and communication technologies and the continued expansion of service industries as the principal sources of jobs. The labor force has become more diverse, with marked increases in the number of women, non-white and immigrant workers, and older workers, and growing divides between people with different amounts of education. Ideological changes have supported these structural changes, with shifts toward greater individualism and personal accountability for work and life replacing notions of collective responsibility.

The decline of job quality results in large part from the greater power of employers relative to workers; the deregulation of labor markets and business friendly government policies have enabled employers to use their resources to make work contingent on their needs as they search for flexibility and ways to reduce costs. The continued decline of unions in the U.S. has both resulted from the kinds of macro changes discussed earlier (such as globalization and technological change) and, in turn, facilitated them. The weakening of unions is intimately related to the reduction in protections for the semi-skilled workers in manufacturing occupations that formed the backbone of the post-World War II U.S. middle class.

The rise in precarious work also reflects the widespread retrenchment and restructuring of social welfare and legal protection systems. The risks and responsibility of many social insurance programs have been shifted away from the government and employers to individuals and their families, resulting in greater economic insecurity.

These two dimensions of low job quality—low wages and benefits, and more job and economic insecurity—underscore the need for policies to protect workers by means of revised social welfare and labor laws as well as to create more good jobs and fewer bad jobs.

The Research Evidence

There is strong evidence that there has been a decline in job quality in the United States since the late 1970s. Labor force surveys and administrative records show that wages have stagnated, income inequality has increased, and there has been a rise in low-wage jobs.

Market incomes (before taxes and benefits) for the average working-age U.S. adult actually fell between 1980 and 2014, reversing the strong upward trend of previous decades. Moreover, the incidence of low-wage and very low-wage jobs grew, spectacularly so for young workers (age eighteen through thirty-four) with less than a college degree. The poverty-wage share even increased for workers with a college degree. Young workers also experienced sizable declines in their median wages (men after 1979, women after around 2000). Declines in nonwage benefits such as employer-paid health insurance and pensions have also been greater for lower-wage workers, another source of rising absolute and relative inequality in job quality.

Changes in the terms of work has been studied mainly by whether or not employment relations are *standard* or characterized by "permanent" open-ended contracts, with full-time work directed by an employer at the employer's place of business and providing regular pay and benefits. *Nonstandard* employment relations, on the other hand, depart from one or more of these terms of employment. Temporary and usually short-term employment replace "permanent" contracts, creating job insecurity. Work is often done at sites other than the employer's, such as temps who work at client organizations rather than at their employing temp agency. The evidence indicates that attachment to an employer has declined, both in terms of less time spent working for a particular employer and more employer changes.

There has especially been a rise in independent contracting, in which individuals are not employees, but are considered to be individual "firms." Estimates of how much of an increase there has been in independent contracting is complicated by the fact that people often engage in this activity as a supplement to their main job and may thus not be counted in many government surveys. Employers also may misclassify persons as independent contractors rather than as employees, as this reduces their costs and their responsibilities for workers. A specific form of independent contracting that has received a great deal of attention in recent years is "gig" work, which refers to work that is mediated by online platforms, such as Uber, Lyft, DoorDash, or TaskRabbit. The incidence of gig work in the overall labor force is low (though rapidly growing), and it is unclear how many people work in such arrangements as their primary job. But such work is problematic in that gig workers are not covered by labor laws such as workers' compensation, unemployment insurance, and other important protections.

Some nonstandard jobs may be good ones, such as well-paid consultants who have a great deal of control over the terms and conditions of work. Others are characterized by low pay, low security, poor working conditions, high anxiety, and poor mental and physical health. However, the quality of nonstandard jobs should be judged in relation to the job quality of standard employment relations. In particular, the shifting of risks from employers to workers has reduced protections for standard workers as well, leading to a stagnation or deterioration of wages for many who are employed on a "permanent" basis.

Recommendations and Solutions

The decline in job quality is reflected in wage stagnation and inequality, and the rise of nonstandard work (along with the general worsening of standard employment relations). The growth of low-paid and uncertain and insecure jobs underlies many social and economic problems, such as reduced economic development, difficulties in family formation and social integration, more poverty and inequality, and a general decline in individual well-being. The realization that falling job quality is linked to so many other problems has helped to put this age-old concern on the front burner for social scientists and policymakers in the United States and around the world. Policies to create good jobs and make bad jobs better are enacted at the organizational level, in firms and workplaces. These organizational policies, in turn, are shaped within the context of labor laws and social welfare institutions and policies.

Job quality differs among countries due to differences in labor market and social welfare protection institutions as well as cultural norms and practices regarding gender, family, age, and so on. These mediate and shape how countries have liberalized their labor markets and restructured their social welfare protections to cope with similar political and economic forces unleashed by an increasingly global and technology-driven economy, as well as by constraints on state budgets produced by slowdowns in economic growth coupled with the aging of labor forces and more diversity in what labor forces need to be productive.

The United States, which is characterized by the dominance of market and financialization decisions in how work is organized and rewarded, has relatively weak institutions to help workers navigate the changing terms and nature of work. The long-term decline of unions and workers' collective bargaining power has been associated with the loss of social protections such as health insurance and retirement benefits. The legacy of employer-delivered health care and retirement support has left people dependent on particular kinds of employment relationships for these basic benefits. There are relatively few active labor market policies that help workers to be retrained and navigate the pathways between jobs, leading to job insecurity and wage stagnation and deterioration. Moreover, regulatory and legal practices and policies associated with work have traditionally been based on the notion of a standard employment relation, which fails to recognize the significance of the rise of nonstandard employment relations, especially of independent contractors who do not have employment relations at all. Labor market institutions need to change to reflect these changes in work arrangements.

Institutions make a big difference in reversing the trends toward wage stagnation and inequality, and the negative consequences of nonstandard work. It is possible to adopt institutional or policy arrangements that generate far more equitable and efficient outcomes than are currently observed in the United States. First, we need policies to protect workers from the two major risks created by changes in the terms of work: job insecurity (both on a specific job and in the ability to find employment elsewhere) and economic insecurity. Second, we need to increase the wages for low-wage jobs. This would lift many workers out of poverty and near-poverty as well as reduce inequality in wages.

The following list outlines several of the kinds of policies that are needed to protect workers and to enhance the qualities of their jobs. The first three are governmental actions at local and national levels. The fourth depends more on managers' decisions as to how to organize the terms and nature of work.

- Separate basic social and economic protections from the labor market and type of work arrangement. Political scientists and sociologists call this "decommodification," in which a person's economic security is not dependent on their labor market participation. Universally available health care, for example, would enable people to make work-related decisions without being worried about having this basic need fulfilled. This is especially important given the trend toward automation of many jobs, which is likely to eliminate routine jobs often held by older workers. While fears of a "jobless future" and the "end of work" are not new (such concerns were also raised in the 1950s and early 1960s, for example), and are likely to be as overstated now as earlier, they do point to the limitations of a system where benefits are delivered through employers (and have spurred a revival of calls for a "Universal Basic Income," for example).
- Labor laws are needed that recognize that the standard employment relationship is no longer the dominant frame for protecting and

regulating work arrangements. For example, efforts by "independent contractors" to organize and collectively bargain with platform companies such as Uber or Lyft are presently hampered by antitrust laws prohibiting single "firms" from colluding, except in special circumstances. The updating of labor laws to counter businesses' misclassification of employees as independent contractors is also necessary. Also necessary are social welfare policies that recognize the diversity of work arrangements, and so make unemployment benefits or workers' compensation more widely available.

- Greater availability of, and access to, education and training, including retraining and lifelong learning, is necessary for people to acquire the skills and knowledge to succeed in a changing economy. Community colleges can play a major role in teaching the skills required of workers and updating them via lifelong learning. Such institutions are more closely aligned with the needs of particular communities and local areas than four-year colleges, and so are more amenable to establishing relationships with particular companies.

- Organizational policies need to recognize the diverse needs and preferences of workers. While everyone wants a good job (though they might define this in different ways), they may well differ in their preferred work arrangement. The labor force is becoming increasingly more diverse with respect to gender, race, age, family status, immigration status, and so on, and managers' organizational policies need to recognize this diversity. For example, some workers (such as women with young children) might wish to work part-time or on a temporary basis if they were able to have control over their work schedules, and to receive benefits (such as health insurance) from their employers that are only available to full-time workers.

Achieving the Needed Objectives

Enacting and implementing these kinds of policies require the coordinated efforts of government, business, and labor. There are of course many obstacles to such endeavors: ideological disagreements about the appropriate role of government in labor markets; a lack of trust in the government and institutions in general; lobbyists trying to obtain favorable regulations for their clients; and businesses wanting to cut costs. The current weakness of the labor movement is related to all of these things, and is the main factor preventing workers from having a voice and being a countervailing force to business and pressuring the government to enact worker-friendly policies.

Implementing the kinds of political governmental policies discussed depends on workers being able to have a real voice in decision-making and to exercise collective agency in the United States. The revitalization of unions is essential to this goal and hinges on the ability to reverse the anti-union climate in the U.S. and to build a more hospitable environment for workers to join unions and benefit from their presence. Labor laws also need to be more supportive of collective bargaining, such as ending forced arbitration in employment contracts.

A new worker movement needs to adapt to the changing terms and organization of work. More than eight in ten persons now work in the service economy in the U.S. This sector is heterogeneous: on the one hand, there are large consumer bureaucracies (such as Walmart or Amazon) that have diverse occupations and so an effective organizing model might be the industrial model illustrated by the Congress of Industrial Organizations (CIO). Here, the "service triangle" of business, labor, and consumers offers possibilities to engage in consumer politics (as opposed to production politics) in which consumers can be mobilized to put pressure on employers to improve the working conditions of workers. The service sector is also characterized by highly skilled occupations (both professionals of various kinds and skilled crafts) that span firms; these workers are more effectively organized via an occupational craft model (such as the American Federation of Labor, or AFL) in which worker power is achieved by control over valued skills.

Unions are effective to the extent they are able to bargain collectively with employers. Collective bargaining coverage is not always equated with union membership, however, as demonstrated in countries such as France that have relative low union membership but high collective bargaining coverage. The most fruitful form of collective bargaining in the U.S. in the future is likely to be sectoral bargaining between firms and workers in particular industries (and perhaps regions). Firm-level bargaining as traditionally practiced in the U.S. is not likely to be effective in view of the reduced attachment of employees to particular firms. Rather, sectoral bargaining (such as that practiced in Denmark or Germany) would help to ensure that firms in the same industrial sector are not disadvantaged competitively by improving the wages of their workers. The U.S. Congress is not likely to approve European-style industry-wide bargaining any time soon, however, and U.S. unions are too weak to pressure employers to adopt it.

An alternative approach to increasing wages is via wage boards, as illustrated by the one established in New York by Governor Andrew

Cuomo, which held hearings and decided that the minimum wage should be $15 in New York City and $12.50 upstate. At least several other states (Arizona, Colorado, California, New Jersey) also have legislation on the books allowing for constituting such boards on the basis of industries or occupations. Another exemplar is the standards board created by the Seattle city council to set pay and working conditions for 30,000 domestic workers.

New forms of worker power are also needed that provide alternatives to unions. For example, "Fight for 15" was able to garner sufficient media attention and pressure state and local governments to increase wages for fast food workers; it was sponsored by the Service Employees International Union (SEIU), though many of the fast food workers who benefited from this effort were not union members. Fight for 15 has now spread well beyond the fast food industry and offers the potential to provide a model to make the service sector the basis for a new middle class, just as the manufacturing sector was the backbone of the post-World War II middle class.

Worker advocacy groups organized at the local level are illustrated by LAANE (Los Angeles Alliance for a New Economy), a coalition of unions, community groups, clergy, immigrant groups, African Americans, Asians, and Latinos. Its goal is to change politics by building power from the bottom; it has won a wage of $15.37 for Los Angeles hotel workers and is pushing for living wages in industries such as construction, recycling and waste hauling, and retail.

Finally, businesses can enhance the quality of jobs as well as their own performance by paying adequate wages and providing workers with opportunities for dignity. Here, managerial ideologies have a strong impact on the behavior of organizations. For example, the shareholder model (in which organizations make decisions based only on the interests of their shareholders as opposed to other stakeholders such as their workers or communities) is a fairly recent development in the U.S., having emerged in the 1980s. While it really only applies to large organizations that are publicly traded, it nevertheless created a frame of thinking about who can make legitimate claims on the profits made by the firm. The recent call by the Business Roundtable to return to a stakeholder model is a promising first step in this direction, though whether this is simply a public relations effort rather than a real change in managerial thinking remains to be seen.

The deterioration in job quality in the United States since the late 1970s has resulted from structural transformations in the economy and has had negative consequences for individuals' and families' work and nonwork lives. Tackling the sources and consequences of this decline in job quality will enhance both the competitiveness of the U.S. economy and the quality of work experienced by workers.

Key Resources

Cappelli, Peter. 1999. *The New Deal at Work: Managing the Market-Driven Workforce*. Boston, MA: Harvard Business School Press.

Clawson, Dan. 2003. *The Next Upsurge: Labor and the New Social Movements*. Ithaca, NY: Cornell University Press.

Doellgast, Virginia, Nathan Lillie, and Valeria Pulignano (eds). 2018. *Reconstructing Solidarity: Labour Unions, Precarious Work, and the Politics of Institutional Change in Europe*. Oxford, UK: Oxford University Press.

Greenhouse, Steven. 2019. *Beaten Down, Worked Up: The Past, Present and Future of American Labor*. New York: Penguin Random House.

Hacker, Jacob S. 2006. *The Great Risk Shift: The Assault on American Jobs, Families, Health Care, and Retirement and How You Can Fight Back*. New York: Oxford University Press.

Howell, David R. 2019. "From Decent to Lousy Jobs: New Evidence on the Decline in American Job Quality, 1979–2017." Working Paper, Washington Center for Equitable Growth.

Howell, David R. and Arne L. Kalleberg. 2019. "Declining Job Quality in the United States: Explanations and Evidence." *RSF: Russell Sage Foundation Journal of the Social Sciences: Changing Job Quality: The Rise of Low-Wage Jobs and Nonstandard Work Arrangements* 5(4): 1–53.

Jacoby, Sanford M. 2001. "Risk and the Labor Market: Societal Past as Economic Prologue." pp. 31–60 in Ivar Berg and Arne L. Kalleberg (eds), *Sourcebook of Labor Markets: Evolving Structures and Processes*. New York: Kluwer Academic/Plenum Publishers.

Kalleberg, Arne L. 2011. *Good Jobs, Bad Jobs: The Rise of Polarized and Precarious Employment Systems in the United States, 1970s–2000s*. New York: Russell Sage Foundation, American Sociological Association Rose Series in Sociology.

Kalleberg, Arne L. 2018. *Precarious Lives: Job Insecurity and Well-Being in Rich Democracies*. Cambridge, UK: Polity Press.

SECTION VI

Looking Forward

SEVENTEEN

The Contested Construction of Social Problems

Stephen Pfohl

All responses to social problems are mediated by the contexts in which they are socially constructed. Effective social constructions bestow a taken-for-granted character upon the stories they tell about why problems occur and what to do about them. This can make certain approaches to social problems appear commonsensical, blessing particular viewpoints on social trouble while cursing others. As such, both social problems and strategies aimed at their amelioration are forever entangled in contested fields of power and knowledge. Although what is considered a problem varies in different times and places, contested social constructions are not merely relative. Nothing is merely relative. Like all aspects of life, constructions of social problems are complex, relational, and systemic. They are produced in dynamic fields of power where first-hand experience and the stories people tell about what troubles them fold recursively back into each other.

How exactly are constructions of social problems shaped by the contexts in which they are produced and contested? And how might reckoning with the contextual framing of social problems contribute to struggles for social justice as we enter the third decade of the twenty-first century? In exploring these questions, this chapter draws attention to four interdependent vectors of influence on how some aspects of troubled social life, rather than others, come to be understood as social problems— *natural historical materiality*, *social psychic subjectivity*, *practices of power*, and *ritual configurations of knowledge*. The chapter concludes with a brief overview of *power-reflexive approaches* to social problems that locate participants, theorists, activists, and policymakers within the troubled social and historical spheres to which they belong.

The Natural Historical Materiality of Social Problems

A focus on the natural historical materiality of contested constructions of social problems explores the influence of a society's dominant mode of economic production on how that society understands behaviors or conditions that are considered problematic. This is an aspect of what Marx and Engels meant by historical materialism. Constructed understandings of social problems are no exception. No matter the troubled behavior or condition—be it gendered violence, racialized policing, corporate malfeasance, religious discrimination, political corruption, the plight of refugees, or drone strikes against suspected terrorists in distant lands—whether or not something is viewed as a social problem is affected by its location within complex economic systems that privilege the wellbeing of some groups, classes, or castes of people over that of others. To the victors go the spoils!

The role played by economic circumstance in shaping constructed viewpoints on social problems is of particular importance today. This is because few aspects of contemporary life remain untouched by capital-intensive economic forces that couple the wealth of some with the impoverishment of others. In this regard, it is important to remember that struggles for economic advantage are never independent of the gendered, racialized, sexualized, and religiously imagined forces with which they intersect in history. The economy, in other words, is not some abstract entity. It is produced, reproduced, or contested in the intersectional ritual practices that shape our embodied experiences of gender, race, sexuality, religion, and so forth. This is a vital but also a limited theoretical insight. Despite the importance of economic forces in shaping our imaginations of social trouble, why something is viewed as a social problem is rarely the result of restrictive economic influence alone. This is because human history is part of a larger *natural history*—a history of the evolving ecology of life in all its complexity. Humans participate in this natural history but never as unencumbered commanders. As such, social problems are forever shaped by two distinct but interconnected forms of economic struggle—*restrictive economic struggle* over who benefits (or is harmed) by a given mode of production and *general economic struggle* over how to intimately inhabit the movement of nature in time.

Restrictive economic struggle is today amplified by profit-driven capitalist technologies that dissect the world with an eye to the bottom line. Think, for instance, of the fossil fuel industry. Oil and gas companies have long lobbied against public recognition of human manufactured climate change as a life-threatening social problem. The same is true of the cigarette industry. For decades, cigarette manufacturers buried evidence of smoking's dangers to health, while funding deceptive advertising campaigns aimed at attracting new smokers. Inequitable economic interests are also a driving force behind recent "populist" campaigns targeting immigrants, people of color, resistive women, and the so-called "fake news" media. Resentful rhetorical outbursts by economically threatened sectors of White working-class America underscore what's at stake—complicity with (or resistance to) a masculinized neo-liberal capitalist will to economic accumulation rooted in avarice, genocidal colonial conquest, and the haunting legacy of the Black Atlantic slave trade. *Stop the invaders! Curtail white genocide! They will not replace us!*

Restrictive economic forces set parameters for social problems nearly everywhere; everywhere, that is, where dreams of monetized advantage spur narcissistic phantasms of a market-worthy self. Dreams of economic domination and the nightmares such dreams create for others are today amplified by information-based cybernetic technologies of various sorts. Cybernetics denotes processes of command, control, and communication between humans and computing machines of many sorts. Lodged at the core of a vast array of economic, scientific, political, military, and cultural initiatives, cybernetic control technologies are an omnipresent feature of contemporary social life. Rising to prominence during the second half of the twentieth-century during a time of cold warfare, by the early twenty-first century, high-speed cybernetic flows of networked information have become the stuff of everyday life. Cybernetic control processes are also a material aspect of the natural historical context in which social problems are today socially constructed. Indeed, whether in the form of smart phones, omnipresent surveillance, data-banking, algorithmic killing machines, or emotional interactions with online video streams, contemporary cybernetic technologies modulate both social psychic experience and how people imagine the problems that trouble them. By framing problems in certain ways but not others, digital cybernetic technologies help solidify (or challenge) profit-driven economic hierarchies.

Symbolic linguistic technologies are key to cybernetic processes of social construction—attention-grabbing news stories and blogs, photos and videos, sound tracks, social media posts and tweets. *Build the wall! Lock her up! Send her back!* Technologies of affect are important as well—suggestive technologies that induce contagious waves of fascinating or fearful emotional resonance or dissonance. The restrictive economic consequences of capital-intensive media technologies are easy to recognize: namely, a massive upward transfer of material benefits for the wealthy at the expense of nearly everyone else. But as inequitable as profit-driven communicative technologies have proved to be in the restrictive economic realm, when deflecting attention from the industrial origins of today's global climate crisis, suggestive cybernetic media may presage something even more catastrophic in the general economic realm—planetary ecological collapse and the extinction of life as we know it.

Reflexive attention to how we are positioned within dynamic social webs of restrictive and general economic force can facilitate a justice-oriented assessment of competing constructions of social problems. Who benefits by dominant ways of imagining social problems? Who is injured or ignored? Questions such as these guide justice-oriented approaches to what counts or should count as a social problem. Attention to the subjective experience of people struggling to define and respond to social problems is a focal point for the next section.

Social Psychic Subjectivity and Social Problems

Social psychic subjectivity concerns the varieties of experience enabled or blocked by communicative social rituals. This too is a factor in the construction of social problems—social psychological processes that lead some people to interpret troubled social life as the result of structured conflict but others to view trouble as evidence of the moral, psychological, biological, or cultural deficiencies of problematic individuals or social groups. To reckon with how it is that people experience troubled social relations in different and sometimes even diametrically opposed ways is to engage with questions about how forces affecting social psychic experience shape subjective perceptions of problems in contexts of social strife.

Social psychic subjectivity is rooted in the symbolic character of our human animal natures. Humans are a precarious species of animals. Like other species, we need to establish stable relations to our environment simply to meet basic needs for food, shelter, sexual procreation, and so forth. Unlike other animal species, however, humans lack innate or biologically imprinted mechanisms for social survival. This puts us at a deficit in comparison to other animal species. To compensate we rely on technology. Technology is fundamental to human social existence. It is rooted in our bodily dispositions without being biologically determined. Moreover, by virtue of a highly developed central nervous system, we humans carry within ourselves the possibilities for what is perhaps our most important technology—language.

Language is a symbolic technology, an instrument for constructing social order through the ritualized use of signs, images, and gesture. As a social technology, language enables us to classify the world and our position within it in meaningful ways. Rooted in our bodily capabilities, language enables us to reduce the chaos of experiential flux to relatively stable categories of cultural meaning. This is crucial for human animal survival. Without language we would have neither a stable social environment nor stable selves. Troubled social interaction challenges the normative confines of language and disrupts subjective experience. In response, symbolic constructions of social problems labor to quell challenges posed by trouble and to assist people in reordering their disrupted social selves.

Language, however, is always sacrificial. It directs meaningful attention to some aspects of life while deflecting attention from others. Language endows our social relations and selves with meaning. But it also separates scripted symbolic understandings from the natural historical complexity of what is real. Things that are real but which lie beyond the confines of language elide consciousness. They exist in the realm of affect but are not symbolically apprehended. They escape linguistic confinement but remain a real—if unconscious—aspect of social psychic experience. This means that social constructions of social problems are haunted by affective aspects of disturbances that exceed symbolic constraint but which are nevertheless felt in the flesh. As such, when examining how social problems are experientially framed in certain ways (but not others) it is essential to reckon with both conscious (linguistic) as well as unconscious (affective) social psychic forces.

When making connections between social psychic subjectivity and the construction of social problems in contemporary digital culture it is important to pay attention to mutations in human experience sparked by high-speed global networks of cybernetic feedback. Commonly envisioned as a data-driven mode of instrumental rationality, cybernetics also operates in a decidedly more expressive manner, casting its spell on social psychic subjectivity like an enchanted two-way mirror. On one side, technological *feedback loops* of information double down on the panoptic capacities of modern power, extending the reach of disciplinary social institutions and surveillance capitalism into the fibers of everyday social life. This is a feature of ramped-up cybernetic control processes—the scanning of algorithmic databanks for signs of social advantage and suspected nonconformity. But amplified data-capture is but a single side of cybernetics' two-way mirror. On the other side lies cybernetics' capacity to suggestively steer streams of meaning and affect, altering perception and the ways we imagine social problems. With this in mind, let us turn to how ritual practices of power confer an aura of believability on certain social constructions, while making others appear false or even unimaginable.

The Contested Power of Social Construction

The word *power* is derived from the Latin verb *potere,* meaning, "to be able." A dynamic characteristic of all social relations, power is the ability to make things happen. As a transformative social force, power enables and constrains. It opens privileged pathways into some regions of social psychic experience while closing the door upon others. Sociology's most consistent understanding of power is derived from Max Weber. It pictures power as the ability to exercise one's will even when others resist. This definition is especially useful when reckoning with the construction of social problems in hierarchical societies. In top-down societies, such as our own, advantaged groups weaponize valuable resources that are used against those they subordinate. This is an important but somewhat limited understanding of power. In what follows, I endeavor to supplement this conception in several ways: first, by conceiving power as a dynamic field of intersectional forces rather than a resource that can be possessed; second, by distinguishing between hegemonic and coercive practices of power; and third, by imagining Northwestern practices of power—including dominant economic, gendered, and racialized expressions of power—as haunted by a continuing *global coloniality of power.*

To conceive of power as a contested field of forces is to imagine a dynamic network of social relations in tension with each other. Within this complex network, some relations amplify other relations, while others resist or struggle to curtail the influence of others. This is to theorize power as a relational field that privileges certain social strata while disadvantaging others. Within this field, relations fold into each other in interactive ways. What is at stake here is not the ownership of willful influence over others but the contested circuits of force to which we are socially bound. Viewing power as a field of contested forces also shifts the locus for interventions into social problems away from questions about who has (or doesn't have) power to concerns with how best to strategically reconfigure the fields of force in which we are situated. Imagining power as a contested social field resonates with various strands of contemporary critical thought, including feminism, critical race theory, poststructuralism, and postcolonial theory. Despite notable differences between these perspectives, together they view power as a dynamic field of forces that affects all aspects of social life.

Fields of power vary in different historical times and places. Moreover, while it is theoretically possible to imagine reciprocal fields of power where the ability to make things happen is distributed in an equitable manner, mutual relations of this sort are today relatively uncommon. Quite the opposite: whether in the private sphere or public life, hierarchical fields of power appear to be the norm nearly everywhere. When most effective, top-down fields of force can make inequitable social relations seem timeless and fixed. But this is not the only thing that power does. Power also engenders resistance, spurring those it subordinates to push back against the fields of force that constrain them. This makes all constructions of social problems contested social constructions. It also leads to a second concern with how power affects the construction of social problems—differences between *coercive* and *hegemonic* practices of power.

Coercive fields of power are brutal. Whether deployed by authoritarian political regimes, gangs of thugs, bloodthirsty conquerors, or democratic governments in torturous places of confinement, such as Abu Ghraib or Guantanamo Bay, coercive power propagates certain socially constructed worldviews, while suppressing others. Violence, the terroristic threat of violence, and torture—these are weapons in the arsenal of coercive power. Hegemonic power, on the other hand, involves the seduction or engineering of consent. Hegemony refers to the ritual production of commonsensical viewpoints on social problems. When most effective, hegemony *naturalizes* contested relations of unequal power. Why do those disadvantaged by hierarchical fields of power occasionally embrace social constructions that subordinate them? Inquiry into this matter is crucial for critical analyses of how practices of power reinforce (or challenge) taken-for-granted understandings of social problems.

Coercion and hegemony bend or distort reality. Failure to reckon with a continuing *coloniality of power* has a related effect. This is because legacies of colonialism and Black Atlantic slavery haunt virtually all aspects of contemporary society—from how we make sense of race and ethnicity to competing definitions of value, success, love, pleasure, gender, sexuality, warfare, and, of course, social problems. This is to recognize that, while few formal colonies remain today, global social life in its contested complexities is not yet fully decolonized. As such, to reckon with social problems in an ethically informed manner, we must reckon simultaneously with the lingering scars of entangled colonial divisions that bifurcate our understandings of self and other, mind and body, economy and culture, life and death.

Power—with its coercions, hegemonies, and continuing colonialities—functions as a dynamic terrain in which contested constructions of social problems are produced, resisted, and changed. To understand why it is that some troubled relations (but not others) are viewed as social problems we must first grapple with the complexities of power at a given moment in history. This enables us to better discern the effects of specific constructions of social problems and what to do about them. What aspects of our troubled social relations do particular constructions cast a light upon? And which do they keep in the dark? With these questions in mind, let's turn to a fourth vector of influence on the construction of social problems—*ritual configurations of knowledge*.

Ritual Configurations of Knowledge

Power and knowledge are reciprocal. Each influences the form and content of the other. And just as multiple forms of power bear upon the ritual construction of social problems, so do multiple varieties of knowledge. To know something is to apprehend, perceive, or understand a given phenomenon, to categorize or classify the thing in question. Most analyses of social construction, however, conceptualize knowledge in strictly cognitive symbolic terms. While important, cognitive approaches by themselves fail to reckon with the complexity of how people come to understand what troubles them as a social problem. As such, restricting analyses of knowledge to cognition limits our understanding of how specific social constructions appeal to those whose attention they captivate. For this reason, it is important to become attuned to forms of knowledge that supplement that provided by cognitive apprehension. These include narrative, emotional, bodily, moral, aesthetic, sacrificial, and haunted modalities of knowledge. In order to gain a more nuanced understanding of the role played by knowledge in shaping constructions of social problems, I will briefly discuss each of these additional ritual pathways into making sense of the world modalities. In combination with cognition, attention to these additional modalities of knowledge provides a more holistic understanding of why it is that people knowingly embrace some socially constructed frameworks but reject others.

Multiple pathways of knowledge frequently work in concert. This strengthens the appeal of a particular social construction. At other times, various modalities of knowledge may be at odds with each other. This weakens a construction's ability to mediate social reality.

Consider, for instance, competing forms of knowledge at play when pondering whether or not immigration should be viewed as a social problem. When framed in strictly cognitive terms, debates pertaining to immigration focus on disagreements about policies and/or principles; disagreements, for instance, about whether undocumented people in the U.S. should be able to apply for citizenship or whether refugees fleeing violence elsewhere should be granted asylum.

In addition to framing questions in purely cognitive terms, competing constructions of immigration as a social problem are propelled by conflicting stories or narratives. Narrative forms of knowledge tell us why people do the things they do and how events unfold in time. Supplementing classificatory cognitive expressions of knowledge, stories stimulate our imaginations and offer us characters to imaginarily identify with and/or oppose. Why, for instance, do large numbers of people from Central America wish to immigrate to the U.S.? In keeping with protectionist narratives of immigration, the story goes something like this: Migrants from south of the border come to the U.S. to take advantage of its job market and welfare system, and this harms "native born" U.S. citizens. When most effective, this narrative renders other stories about why many Central Americans seek refuge in the U.S. null and void. The story is told differently, however, by those who picture the U.S. as a country built by immigrants or critics who attribute the plight of Central American refugees to instabilities in the region brought about in large measure by U.S. support for authoritarian political regimes during the second half of the twentieth century. From the viewpoint of these counter-narratives, immigration appears less a problem than ill-conceived border control policies that erect storied walls against contradictory historical actualities.

Emotional forms of knowledge also play a role in the effective ritual construction of social problems. Think, for instance, of recent political efforts to stoke fear of immigrants as parasites, violent criminals, foreign invaders, or Trojan horse terrorists. Affectively charged knowledge claims such as these serve as tactical weapons in the arsenal of fearful Whites waging war against immigration as social problem. Here heart-felt modalities of knowledge cross paths with a continuing coloniality of power, inducing feelings of fear, defensiveness, and sometimes even hatred. On the other side, mobilizing sympathetic emotions on the part of those who identify with the dreams of immigrants or who empathize with the plight of refugees is a valuable resource in the toolkit of activists who view punitive border control policies as the true problem affecting immigration.

Bodily ways of knowing also play a role in why people identify with certain social constructions rather than other ways of making sense of social trouble. A somatic effect of powerful social constructions, knowledge can sensuously congeal in the flesh in ways that defy words. For alarmist control agents and citizens frightened by emotionally charged anti-immigrant propaganda, the mere proximity of brown-skinned Spanish-speaking people can arouse states of nervousness, irritability, or anger. The opposite may be true for people whose hearts are aligned with pro-immigration constructions promoting compassion for refugees seeking sanctuary.

Moral and aesthetic inflections of knowledge are likewise factors in the ritual construction of social problems. Constructions that distinguish social problems from normal forms of social life inevitably shade the differences they analyze in moral tones. Morally feeling that things are right or wrong represents another modality of knowledge that influences how people respond to competing social constructions. Sometimes putative moral knowledge is explicit. Protectionists warn, for instance, that unchecked immigration poses a moral problem. It exposes the country to a lot of "bad hombres." Everyone, we are told, knows this to be true except "bleeding-heart liberals" and "dupes of political correctness." By contrast, those who view dehumanizing border protection policies as the real social problem understand ethical issues raised by immigration in decidedly different terms. Aesthetic forms of knowledge also help shape how social problems are imagined. Aesthetic forms of knowledge bless certain ways of behaving or certain types of people as beautiful, while condemning others as repulsive or ugly. This often takes place at an unconscious level. Which do you find more beautiful—a fortified border wall or migrants struggling for a better future? How you answer this question may indicate where you stand on immigration as a social problem.

All knowledgeable social constructions are selective and mediated by power. With this in mind, it is important to ask about what is ritually sacrificed by effective configurations of cognitive, narrative, emotional, bodily, moral, and aesthetic knowledge about putative social problems. What is sacrificed, excluded, or overlooked by a given social construction is itself a constitutive aspect of that construction. All constructions are partial and defined in part by what they leave out. This is evident when confronting questions about immigration. To construct an understanding of immigration from one side of the border but not the other or to take a stance on immigration that is emptied of history—this is to ignore important pieces of the puzzle that make immigration such a pressing contemporary concern. That which is repressed or kept from sight by a particular social construction does not, however, cease to exist simply because it escapes our conscious attention. What is repressed instead inevitably returns to haunt, disturb, or subvert the supposed naturalness of a given social construction. As a result, even the most inclusive constructions are haunted by sacrifices and silences. This means that all social constructions are partial. None escape the natural historical fields of power and resistance in which they are at once forged and contested. The implications of this inherent partiality for justice-oriented scholarship and policy initiatives directed at social problems are discussed in the closing section of this chapter.

Power-Reflexive Approaches to Social Problem Construction

Socially constructed understandings of social problems are produced at the contested crossroads of natural historical materiality, social psychic subjectivity, and the intersectional fields of power and knowledge in which people struggle with troubling aspects of social life. In combination, these contextual forces bear upon how societies understand (or fail to understand) repetitive conflicts that disturb them. Where are you and I in this story? Power-reflexive approaches to social problems challenge justice-oriented scholars, policy makers, and activists to locate ourselves in the narratives we tell about problems and how to solve them. To be power-reflexive means to double back upon the contested fields of power and knowledge in which we ourselves are situated. As such, when reckoning with the contextual framing of social problems, power-reflexive approaches invite us to engage critically with the circuits of power and knowledge in which our own claims to knowledge are produced. The chapter concludes with a short meditation on how power-reflexive methods might contribute to social justice-oriented approaches to problem solving.

From a power-reflexive viewpoint, all forms of knowledge, including socially constructed knowledge of social problems, are understood as an active intervention in the world rather than an account offered from the outside looking in. As such, power-reflexive methods of inquiry aim to materially transform—rather than idealistically transcend—the existing matrices of power in which we are historically situated. To accomplish this, it is necessary to double back upon contextual forces at work in the social constructions that influence our own research, policy initiatives, and activism. This is to partially reverse or at least critically supplement the prevalence of seemingly context-free methods of inquiry in contemporary professional social science practice. By contrast, power-reflexive forms of inquiry mirror back the ways that all forms of analytic construction, their own included, are partially and provisionally situated within complex social knots of power.

In closing, I invite you to consider three challenges posed by power-reflexive approaches to justice-oriented social problem construction. The first invites inquiry into how our biographical positions within natural historical fields of power affects what we see (or are unable to see) about social problems. The challenge here is to recognize that our own social psychic subjectivity is embedded in systemic regimes of race, class, sexuality, nation, and religion and that, for better or worse, this influences how we imagine social problems. Reflexive attention to this matter is not easy. It typically involves processes of strategic unlearning, some of which can make us feel awkward, even embarrassed.

Think, for instance, of reflexive concerns raised by social construction pertaining to gendered troubles. Power-reflexive methods call upon us to imagine gender as not only a factor in the construction of social problems but also a place of systemic privilege for cisgender straight men, whether this is consciously recognized or not. This is why it is critical to ask how social psychic blinders produced by rituals of hegemonic masculinity can shade even the best-intentioned accounts of gendered social problems. Here it is important to ask whether what most interests straight-minded men about social problems might seem strange or even worrisome to women or people for whom gender is experienced in non-binary terms. While reckoning with the contested complexities of gender can provoke unease, risking unease is a constitutive feature of power-reflexive inquiry. It encourages us to venture beyond the confines of our social psychic comfort zones. Related discomforts may productively arise when grappling with how racial, class, and nation-based configurations of power warp how we think, feel about, and act in relation to divisive social matters.

Reckoning with discomforts that haunt decontextualized mainstream social science methods is a core aspect of power-reflexive approaches to systemic unlearning (and relearning). Strategies such as this, however, are hardly welcomed with open arms by elite educational institutions, powerful governmental agencies, or nonprofits steeped in the logic of hierarchy. As such, learning to practice power reflexivity may require non-standard approaches to pedagogy, such as creating counter-hegemonic scholarly communities supportive of justice-oriented research and policy initiatives. Cutting against the grain of standardized academic inquiry and the job-market that feeds it, power-reflexive approaches to education challenge us to imagine and implement justice-oriented approaches to reflexive scholarship and activism. Other power-reflexive pedagogies include creating reciprocal connections with communities troubled by systemic social inequities; opening ourselves to histories and cultures other than our own; learning new languages; engaging imaginatively with various forms of art, literature, music, theater, film, video, poetry, and dance; allying with justice-oriented social movements; and learning to interact in a discerning manner with digital technologies at play in the cybernetic social landscape in which we communicate with each other.

A second challenge posed by power-reflexive approaches invites us to reflect upon how our involvement in specific programs of research, social policy, or activism relates to more general systemic configurations of social power. Whether we are engaging with questions pertaining to corporate price-fixing, cross-border sex trafficking, rising suicide rates, or epidemic experiences of anxiety and depression, a power-reflexive sensibility challenges us to make connections between local and global fields of power. In what ways, for instance, might pressures felt by financial traders—including emotional and heart-palpitating pressures—be connected, not only to episodes of corporate malfeasance, but also to rises in income and wealth inequality, variations in the price of oil, or support for the latest war in the Middle East? Would problems associated with price-fixing, insider trading, or even armed robbery be framed differently in a general economic system that is as attentive to equitable reciprocity, mutual care, and ecological sustainability as to restrictive economic advantage? What about problems associated with prostitution and "sex work"? Would sex work exist in the forms that it currently does—or even exist at all—if women had greater economic control over their own lives? Thinking about social problems in such complex and systemic ways is a second challenge posed by power-reflexive approaches.

A third challenge offered by power-reflexive approaches to the construction of social problems involves applying complex lessons about the dynamic ecology of power to the pursuit of a more just society. This need not occur at some grandiose or society-wide level. Indeed, nurturing a power-reflexive sensibility likewise attunes us to injustices much closer to home. As such, it is important to engage with efforts to combat systemic forces of injustice in places where we live and labor. Most of us don't have to travel far to learn this lesson. Think only of the epidemic of underreported sexual assaults taking place on the college campuses where so many of us work or of racialized criminal injustices in the communities in which we reside. When pondering such troubling concerns, it is important to keep in mind that small changes or minor reforms can sometimes spark imaginative transformations of a more systemic sort.

By endeavoring to attune our scholarship to struggles for social justice, power-reflexive approaches to social problem construction encourage the development of a critical sociological imagination. In an age of cybernetic power, this demands a *quality of mind* attuned to the feedback loops of power in which we are ecologically enveloped. This calls upon us to ally our efforts, if modestly, with people everywhere trying to break free of the haunting shadows of social injustice. Practicing reflexivity about power likewise reminds us that social justice always begins in the here and now. In this, power-reflexive methods of social problem construction challenge us to dismantle barriers that all too often separate our scholarly or ethical-political activities from those of our everyday lives. This chapter leaves you with this challenge.

Afterword: America on the Edge: Fighting for a Socially Just World

Michelle Christian

In January 2020 we ushered in a new decade of the twenty-first century and the problems facing U.S. society and our globally, interconnected world seemed profound and stark. We almost went to war with Iran after the U.S. military assassination of Major General Qasem Soleimani. Australia was on fire, with 16 million acres lost in the most devastating wildfire to hit the country, a by-product of global climate injustice. Breaking previous records, in 2019, 76,000 unaccompanied migrant children were captured at the U.S.–Mexico border and 500,000 family units attempted to cross. New figures released by U.S. government officials acknowledged that 5,400 children were separated from their families during the Trump administration's devastating family separation policy. It seemed as if every major city in the U.S. was experiencing a rise of homelessness alongside the fact that the number of Americans lacking health insurance went up. These issues, and the specific themes outlined in this book, demonstrate how our social problems are immediate, material, and interconnected. The United States is on the edge. The edge looks like a loss of safety, a loss of sustainability, a loss of opportunity, a loss of equity, a loss of democracy. So much is at stake and so much is to be gained by learning from our most entrenched social obstacles and initiating purposeful, creative, and just solutions.

The authors in this book expertly do just that. Sociologists and members of The Society for the Study of Social Problems demonstrate our dedication to asking important societal research questions; how we gather empirically rigorous and detailed data; and, lastly, how we apply sophisticated analyses to the issues gripping our nation. Throughout the past year, as we saw heart-wrenching media photos and read news stories of violence, inequity, and powerful actors and institutions that limited rights and social possibility, sociologists were behind the scenes academically studying these problems in depth, with meticulous analyses, and exposing the implications of such social phenomena. Hence, the cross-section of themes covered in this book encompass a range of urgent concerns. Chapters included the manifestation of racial injustices seen through new forms of Islamophobia, anti-immigrant sentiment, and unequal and unjust institutions. Other chapters exposed the erosion of social protection as reflected in weak parental leave policies and limited family law, weakened healthcare access, the lack of affordable housing, and entrenched education inequities. How criminal in(justice) continues to plague us was also uncovered in numerous chapters by highlighting unchecked police violence, the criminalization of immigrants, and the derailing of life chances for those with the mark of a criminal record. The ongoing struggle for social justice guides all of the contributions and demonstrates how much is at stake for all of us.

In addition to acknowledging and researching social problems the goal of this volume was to affirm that social change is possible. Each chapter had a series of concrete actions and practices that can be taken. As sociologists we argue it is necessary and urgent to engage and make claims in the public domain and to use our knowledge to help produce the change that is needed. Policy makers, advocates, and institutional actors can apply the suggestions given and facilitate potential concrete transformation. These suggestions are both large and structural and small and individual.

Robert Aponte reminds us that training in de-escalation techniques has already been successfully implemented in cities such as Dallas, Los Angeles, and Camden to mitigate police killings. Arne Kalleberg calls for new labor laws that acknowledge that jobs are no longer defined by standard employment relationships and hence need to reflect the needs of gig and independent contract workers. Kalleberg poignantly articulates the importance of not linking basic social and economic protections and rights to one's form of work relationship. Reproductive rights are under the greatest assault in a generation, as noted by Sujatha Jesudason. Her suggestions range from allowing oral contraceptives over the counter without prescription to enacting the comprehensive proposals outlined in the Blueprint for Sexual and Reproductive Health, Rights, and Justice. The Blueprint particularly linked reproductive rights to a wide swath of interconnected forces shaping reproductive health such as immigration, racial justice, and LGBTQ liberation. Neil Greene and Wayne Centrone argue that responding to homelessness includes eradicating quality-of-life ordinances that criminalize homelessness to simply building more affordable housing units. Lastly, the environmental crisis we are globally and nationally facing, with climate change and disastrous toxic exposures and pollution, is directly linked to racism and to calls for an environmental justice agenda that is vast and specific. David Pellow's approach is national and international scope. The U.S. should bolster the Environmental Protection Agency's Civil Rights Office and revise the commerce clause of the U.S. Constitution to curtail the outsourcing of trash to poorer nations.

Most poignantly, it is important to acknowledge that our social problems are not too complicated or engrained and that all is not lost. We may be on the edge but we are not over the cliff. We can use our sociological tools to identify problems, understand those problems, and call for solutions. A socially just world is one we strive for, and 2020 is an impactful year. The election cycle has already seen an acknowledgment of entrenched issues that in the past barely received recognition: the need for reparations for African Americans, the possibility of a universal basic income, and a climate agenda demanded by the younger generation, to name just a few. Now more than ever sociologists need to continue to be key voices in national conversations. We have a role to play in classrooms, out in the field, in the corridors of power, and out in the streets.